DYNASTY!

New England's Sixth
NFL Championship

NICKY BRILLOWSKI, *Book Design*
KITTY GRIGSBY, *Cover Design*

ISBN: 978-1-940056-72-2

Printed in the United States of America
KCI Sports Publishing   3340 Whiting Avenue, Suite 5   Stevens Point, WI 54481
Phone: 1-800-697-3756   Fax: 715-344-2668
www.kcisports.com

Contents

Introduction

The Dynasty Continues

New England Patriots – World Champions!

It never gets old does it? After having to sit through a year as runner-up the Patriots and their fans are back on top of the NFL throne.

Let the celebration begin!

It is an honor to write an introduction to such a historic season. Led by head coach Bill Belichick and the incomparable Tom Brady this Patriots team fought through adversity all year. After losing back-to-back games in December – an unheard of result throughout New England – many had written this Patriots team off as not up to the challenge. What a mistake. As great teams often do, the Pats peaked at just the right time to earn their way back to another Super Bowl appearance.

The perseverance, teamwork and will to win that made up the DNA of this Patriots team was on full display week after week. In the following pages Dynasty! proudly brings you on a trip down memory lane of this championship season that came to its jubilant conclusion with the Super Bowl victory over a very talented Los Angeles Rams team.

Our heartfelt congratulations go out to Patriots owner Robert Kraft, Coach Bill Belichick and his staff, and the entire team on their incredible accomplishments this season. Celebrate this season Patriots fans, and save this book to revisit the Pats' magical moments and unforgettable team - both stars and role players – who rewarded your faith with yet another NFL Championship.

Congratulations New England!

OPPOSITE: Super Bowl LIII MVP, Julian Edelman.
CHARLIE RIEDEL / AP PHOTO

Brady & Gronk

Future Hall of Famers lead way in opener

Tom Brady and Rob Gronkowski sent New England fans into a panic this offseason when they hinted at retiring rather than returning to the Patriots in 2018.

On Sunday, it was the rest of the NFL watching in fear.

Brady threw for 277 yards and three touchdowns, hitting Gronkowski for 123 yards and a score to lead the defending AFC champions to a 27-20 victory over the Houston Texans. The reigning NFL MVP found Gronkowski seven times, including a 21-yard touchdown three plays after Deshaun Watson fumbled a handoff at the Texans 19 on Houston's first offensive play.

"It's very important that they came out and played the way they did. They're our leaders," said Phillip Dorsett, who had seven catches, including a touchdown. "When they play well, they give an adrenaline boost to the rest of the team."

Brady, 41, clashed with the team he's led to five Super Bowl titles in the past year over the treatment of his personal fitness guru and the plans to elevate backup Jimmy Garoppolo to starter. In February, after throwing for 500 yards in a Super Bowl loss to the Philadelphia Eagles, Brady was coy about returning this season.

The Patriots dangled Gronkowski as trade bait this summer before

SEPT. 9, 2018

PATRIOTS 27
TEXANS 20

FOXBORO, MA
GILLETTE STADIUM

OPPOSITE: Tom Brady gets a lift from David Andrews after throwing a touchdown pass to Rob Gronkowski during the first half.
CHARLES KRUPA / AP PHOTO

BELOW: Dont'a Hightower, left, dives to recover a fumbled handoff by Houston Texans quarterback Deshaun Watson.
CHARLES KRUPA / AP PHOTO

ABOVE: Rob Gronkowski catches a pass between Texans defensive backs Tyrann Mathieu (32) and Kareem Jackson (25) during the second half. Gronkowski fumbled and Mathieu recovered on the play.
CHARLES KRUPA / AP PHOTO

OPPOSITE: Stephon Gilmore, right, intercepts a pass intended for Texans wide receiver Vyncint Smith, obscured behind Patriots cornerback Eric Rowe (25), in the end zone.
CHARLES KRUPA / AP PHOTO

agreeing instead to sweeten his contract with $4.3 million in reachable incentives. Gronkowski reportedly threatened to retire if traded.

"I'm just glad to be here, glad to be part of this team, glad to be part of this organization," he said. "All that talk, all that stuff, I would love to put it in the past."

Brady also found James White for a touchdown, completing 26 of 39 passes in all; he also had an interception on a pass that was tipped at the line of scrimmage. It was Gronkowski's 31st career regular-season or playoff game of 100 yards or more, tying Tony Gonzalez's NFL record.

"We've been playing together for a long time," Brady said. "I know his body language. I know his ability to run and what routes. He can do it. He can do really all the routes. It's just a matter of giving

him a chance, and it came with a big touchdown today."

Watson, who missed the final nine games last season with a torn right ACL, completed 17 of 35 passes for 176 yards, one score and one interception. He struggled to move the team in the first 40 minutes, managing just a pair of field-goal drives before Alfred Blue ran it in from 1 yard to make it 24-13 in the last two minutes of the third period.

A muffed punt by New England's Riley McCarron with under five minutes left set up Watson's 5-yard TD pass to Bruce Ellington and cut the deficit to 27-20. But after getting the ball back at their 1 with 43 seconds left, the Texans failed to reach midfield.

"I think it was terrible, on my part," Watson said. "I just feel like you can put the `L' on me."

With Julian Edelman serving a four-game suspension, Dorsett caught seven passes for 66 yards, including a 4-yard TD pass in the closing seconds of the first half to make it 21-6. White had four receptions for 38 yards, including a 12-yard score.

The Patriots did have trouble with turnovers.

Brady had an interception in the first quarter on a throw tipped by defensive lineman Angelo Blackson and brought in by Tyrann Mathieu at the Patriots 17. The Texans went backward 7 yards before Ka'imi Fairbairn's 42-yard field goal made it 7-3.

Gronkowski also fumbled in the third quarter after a 25-yard reception across the middle. Mathieu recovered, but after advancing to the New England 17, the Texans gave the ball back on downs. The muffed punt by McCarron gave the Texans one last chance.

BOX SCORE

	1	2	3	4	T
HOUSTON	3	3	7	7	20
NEW ENGLAND	7	14	3	3	27

Flat Pats

Jacksonville wins rematch 31-20

Eight months later and with much less on the line, the Jacksonville Jaguars found a way to close out Tom Brady and the New England Patriots.

The significance of it might not be known for some time.

Not even the bold, brash Jaguars would acknowledge it was anything more than a Week 2 win. Others would disagree.

Blake Bortles threw four touchdown passes, three in the first half, and the Jaguars beat Brady and the Patriots 31-20 Sunday in a rematch of last season's AFC championship game.

The victory -- Jacksonville's first in nine tries against Brady -- could signal a new favorite in the AFC.

"Every week is about us," Jaguars All-Pro cornerback Jalen Ramsey said. "We feel like if we're at the top of our game, we can't be beat. They were our opponents, so that's what we prepared for."

Bortles threw for 377 yards in the best game of his five-year career.

He threw perfect TD passes to Donte Moncrief, Keelan Cole and Austin Seferian-Jenkins in the first half, the second time Bortles has accomplished that feat. Bortles sealed the victory with a 61-yard pass to Dede Westbrook in the fourth quarter.

Westbrook took a short pass on a crossing route, made one defender miss and outran another down the sideline and into the end zone. Cole delivered the key block.

Cole finished with seven receptions

SEPT. 16, 2018

JAGUARS 31 PATRIOTS 20

JACKSONVILLE, FL TIAA BANK FIELD

OPPOSITE: Jaguars Donte Moncrief catches a 4-yard touchdown pass over Patriots cornerback Stephon Gilmore.
PHELAN M. EBENHACK / AP PHOTO

BELOW: Tom Brady is tackled by Jacksonville Jaguars Malik Jackson (97) and A.J. Bouye (21) after scrambling for yardage.
PHELAN M. EBENHACK / AP PHOTO

for 116 yards and a score. He made a spectacular, one-handed catch on Jacksonville's second drive and beat Eric Rowe for a 24-yard touchdown three plays later. Rowe was benched.

Westbrook's catch-and-run put the Jaguars (2-0) ahead 31-13, allowing them to start celebrating their second victory in franchise history against New England (1-1) and first in the regular season. They hadn't beaten the Pats since January 1999.

"You have a bad day against a good team, it's a recipe for losing," Brady said. "And we certainly had a bad day."

Brady completed 24 of 35 passes for 235 yards and two touchdowns, both to Chris Hogan. He was sacked twice.

Brady pleaded with teammates on the bench early. Offensive coordinator Josh McDaniels appeared to deliver stern words, too.

Just when the Patriots started showing signs of life -- they were down 11 and in field-goal range early in the fourth quarter -- Dante Fowler stripped Brady. Fowler was making his season debut after being suspended for the season opener.

"We just obviously didn't do anything well enough or close to well enough to be able to take a win today," Pats coach Bill Belichick said. "It's disappointing to have the kind of day that we had today, but that's what it was, so we'll live with it, own it and move on."

ABOVE: Chris Hogan catches a 29-yard touchdown pass during the second half.
PHELAN M. EBENHACK / AP PHOTO

OPPOSITE ABOVE: Jacksonville Jaguars wide receiver Keelan Cole makes a great one-handed catch in front of Patriots defensive back Eric Rowe.
PETER READ MILLER / AP PHOTO

OPPOSITE BELOW: Sony Michel pick up 15 yards on a third quarter run.
JIM MAHONEY / AP PHOTO

BOX SCORE

	1	2	3	4	T
NEW ENGLAND	0	3	7	10	20
JACKSONVILLE	14	7	3	7	31

Student beats the teacher

Patricia gets first win against former team

Matt Patricia beat mentor Bill Belichick, seemingly making all the right moves to help the Detroit Lions defeat the New England Patriots 26-10 Sunday night.

"I'm sure it meant a lot, his first win as a head coach," Detroit quarterback Matthew Stafford said. "Probably no sweeter than to do it against your old team.

"We needed this one."

The Lions (1-2) suddenly looked like a team with a plan on offense and defense under their first-year coach, and former New England assistant. They opened the season with a 31-point loss to the New York Jets at home and fell short in a comeback at San Francisco.

The Patriots (1-2) have had weaknesses exposed on both sides of the ball, losing two of their first three games for the first time since 2012.

The Patriots don't often lose back-to-back games; they entered Sunday night 45-6 after a regular-season loss since 2003. But after a Week 2 clunker against the Jaguars, and then a slow-starting, disjointed performance against the Lions, they've suffered a rare two-game skid.

"We just didn't do anything well enough to give ourselves a chance to win," Belichick said. "Similar situation last week -- get behind early, played from behind and just weren't able to make it up. So, just going to have to work our way out of it. Obviously, we've got a lot of work to do. There's no shortcut, no easy way. Just got to do a better job."

Added safety Devin McCourty: "Right now, it feels like two bad weeks of football."

One of the hallmarks of Belichick's teams over the years has been that they don't beat themselves, but

SEPT. 23, 2018

LIONS 26 PATRIOTS 10

DETROIT, MI FORD FIELD

OPPOSITE: Detroit Lions wide receiver Kenny Golladay scores on a 4-yard touchdown reception in the second quarter. Patriots cornerback Stephon Gilmore defends on the play.
JIM MAHONEY / AP PHOTO

BELOW: Patriots head coach Bill Belichick and Detroit Lions head coach Matt Patricia talk after the game.
PAUL SANCYA / AP PHOTO

ABOVE: Detroit Lions running back Kerryon Johnson tries to break free for extra yardage.
JIM MAHONEY / AP PHOTO

RIGHT: Patriots rookie linebacker Ja'Whaun Bentley is tackled by Detroit Lions tight end Luke Wilson after an interception.
JIM MAHONEY / AP PHOTO

OPPOSITE: James White beats Lions cornerback Quandre Diggs for a 10-yard touchdown reception during the second half.
DUANE BURLESON / AP PHOTO

the 2018 edition has yet to prove it can live up to that standard.

How does a Belichick-coached team get penalized for 12 men on the field on defense?

That's what happened in the loss to the Lions, and it's just bad football.

"It's a mistake," Belichick snapped when asked how the penalty happened. "Did you think it was planned?"

Detroit was in control from the start, creating holes for rookie running back Kerryon Johnson and giving Matthew Stafford time to pass.

Johnson had 101 yards rushing on 16 carries, becoming the first player to reach the mark for the Lions since Reggie Bush ran for 117 yards against Green Bay on Nov. 28, 2013. Detroit's 70-game stretch without a 100-yard rusher was the longest since the NFL-AFL merger.

Tom Brady pulled the Patriots within three points on a 10-yard TD pass to James White early in the third.

Detroit refused to let the five-time Super Bowl-winning quarterback get any closer.

Stafford responded with a 33-yard TD pass, capping a 10-play, 75-yard drive that took more than 6 minutes off the clock.

Darius Slay picked off Brady's pass at the Detroit 15 midway through the fourth quarter, helping the Lions seal the win.

"We're not scoring enough points. We're not executing well enough on a down-by-down basis, certainly at a high level that we should have our expectations set at," Brady said. "There's been a lot of talk about it in practice, it's just not getting done on the field. And we got to get it corrected soon."

BOX SCORE

	1	2	3	4	T
NEW ENGLAND	0	3	7	0	10
DETROIT	3	10	7	6	26

New England Patriots head coach Bill Belichick watches from the sideline during the second half.
ELISE AMENDOLA/ AP PHOTO

Home sweet home

Pats stop skid with rout of Dolphins

The Patriots' losing streak is over.

And so is the Dolphins' undefeated start.

Tom Brady threw for 274 yards and three touchdowns and the New England Patriots handed Miami its first loss of the season in a 38-7 rout on Sunday.

It denied the Dolphins (3-1) their first 4-0 start since Hall of Fame coach Don Shula's last season in 1995.

"I thought we got what we needed from our team today," Patriots coach Bill Belichick said.

Brady improved to 15-1 as a starter against Miami.

"We hadn't played well in the last weeks," Brady said. "This game's great. But you've gotta turn the page."

New England (2-2) may be doing that without one of its best players.

Tight end Rob Gronkowski, one of Brady's favorite targets, left the game in the third quarter with a right ankle injury and did not return.

It put a slight damper on an afternoon in which New England showed the kind of consistency on both sides of the ball that had been missing in back-to-back losses to Jacksonville and Detroit. Since 2002, the Patriots are 8-0 after back-to-back losses.

In its two losses, New England's offense struggled to find its rhythm and sustain drives on third down. It did both Sunday, taking advantage of a Dolphins defense that couldn't seem to match the Patriots' speed.

Running back James White finished with a rushing and receiving touchdown. Rookie running back Sony Michel also rushed 25 times for 112 yards and his first career

SEPT. 30, 2018

PATRIOTS 38
DOLPHINS 7

FOXBORO, MA
GILLETTE STADIUM

OPPOSITE: Phillip Dorsett, right, celebrates his touchdown catch with Cordarrelle Patterson during the first half.
ELISE AMENDOLA / AP PHOTO

BELOW: Miami Dolphins quarterback Ryan Tannehill is sacked for a 9-yard loss by Patriots defensive tackle Adam Butler during third quarter action.
JIM MAHONEY / AP PHOTO

touchdown. It was perfect timing after Rex Burkhead went on injured reserve last week with a neck injury.

Miami struggled in every phase and looked very much like the team that has lost 10 straight road games to New England.

Ryan Tannehill finished 11 for 20 for 100 yards and an interception. He was pulled in the fourth quarter in favor of Brock Osweiler. Osweiler connected with Frank Gore for a 6-yard touchdown pass in the fourth quarter for Miami's lone score.

"Not a lot went right for us," Tannehill said.

Miami was just 3 of 11 on third down and managed only 172 total yards. The Dolphins also had two turnovers and were whistled for 10 penalties, totaling 89 yards.

Miami had a strong start on defense, intercepting Brady on New England's second offensive series.

But following a quick Dolphins' punt, the Patriots bounced back with a 55-yard TD pass from Brady to Cordarrelle Patterson to take a 10-0 lead.

The 55-yard pass was New England's longest play of the season. Patterson caught the pass over his shoulder along the sideline and stutter-stepped past safety T.J.

McDonald to find a clear path to the end zone.

Then about midway through the second quarter, Tannehill fumbled a snap to begin a series that was recovered by Patriots linebacker Kyle Van Noy on the Dolphins 2. White ran it in for a touchdown on the next play to make it 17-0.

The Patriots then ended the half with a 15-play, 85-yard drive capped by an acrobatic touchdown grab in the end zone by Phillip Dorsett.

Dorsett, who had no catches in last week's loss to Detroit, finished with four catches for 55 yards.

Patriots receiver Josh Gordon made his debut Sunday, marking his first playing time in New England since his trade from the Cleveland Browns on Sept. 17.

Gordon made his first reception at the 7:27 mark of the first quarter, hauling in a 13-yard grab.

He finished with two catches for 32 yards.

"I have no doubt I can take advantage of this opportunity," Gordon said. "I'm more than blessed, I'm extremely grateful to be in this scenario. I think the only thing right for me to do is take advantage of it."

ABOVE: Dolphins wide receiver Danny Amendola is upended by Patriots cornerback Jason McCourty, right.

WINSLOW TOWNSON / AP PHOTO

OPPOSITE: James White makes a great catch on a 14-yard touchdown reception in the third quarter.

JIM MAHONEY / AP PHOTO

BOX SCORE

	1	2	3	4	T
MIAMI	0	0	0	7	7
NEW ENGLAND	3	21	7	7	38

The 500 club

Brady reaches 500 TD passes in Pats win

On a night when he reached 500 career touchdown passes, Tom Brady welcomed back a buddy with one of his three scoring tosses Thursday, then connected with a newcomer who could help him reach more milestones.

Brady also sneaked in for a rushing touchdown and the New England Patriots put together their second straight win after a mediocre start to the season, beating Indianapolis 38-24.

Brady's 500th went to Josh Gordon, recently acquired from Cleveland, where he basically was unavailable through NFL suspensions for all but five games over the past three seasons. But, as he often does, Brady spread the wealth, hitting running back James White 10 times for 77 yards, and greeting the return of buddy Julian Edelman by completing seven for 57 yards to him.

"We wanted to get him the ball and he made some great plays," Brady said about Edelman. "Just good to have him out there. We all want it to be perfect when we go out and it was great to have him out there ... healthy and having fun."

As for 500 TD passes, third on the career list behind Peyton Manning (539) and Brett Favre (508), Brady called it a collective mark.

"I think all these things like that, milestones, there are so many people that contribute, all the people that have really worked hard," he said. "A quarterback doesn't throw to himself.

OCT. 4, 2018

PATRIOTS 38
COLTS 24

FOXBORO, MA
GILLETTE STADIUM

OPPOSITE: Josh Gordon, front, goes up high to catch Brady's 500th touchdown pass.
CHARLES KRUPA / AP PHOTO

BELOW: Tom Brady, right, congratulates wide receiver Josh Gordon on catching career touchdown pass number 500.
STEVEN SENNE / AP PHOTO

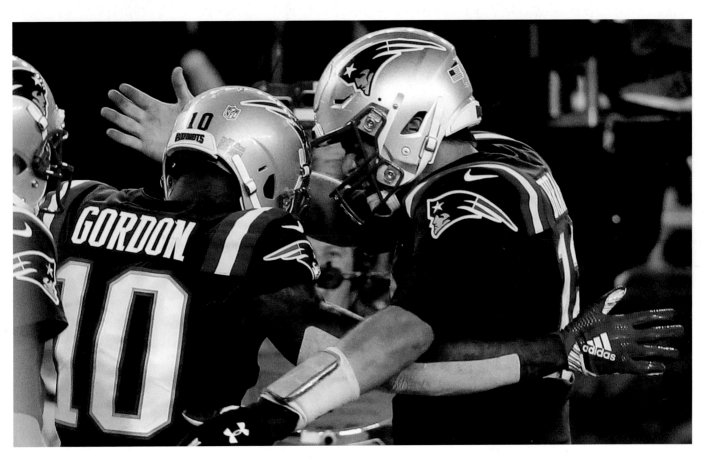

"These are all great team awards, pretty cool."

The five-time NFL champion also tied Colts kicker Adam Vinatieri, a former teammate, for most victories with 226. Brady finished 34 for 44 for 341 yards.

As everyone in Gillette Stadium expected, except apparently the Colts, Brady started off with a pass to Edelman, who was wide open for 9 yards. That drew the first of many loud cheers for the 10th-year veteran receiver in his first game since the 2017 preseason, when he tore up a knee. Edelman was suspended for the first four games this year for violating the NFL's policy on performance enhancers.

"During the rehab you are just sitting there and waiting to get back on the field," Edelman said. "It felt great to be out there with the guys."

That was the first of three receptions for 28 yards for Edelman on the opening 75-yard touchdown drive Brady capped with a 1-yard toss to Cordarrelle Patterson.

From there, even though the Colts (1-4) had a drive deep into New England (3-2) territory, usually reliable Adam Vinatieri missed a 38-yard field goal.

Nothing was going right for Indianapolis, particularly after Brady led a 72-yard march to his sneak from the 1. Then he took the Patriots 68 yards near the end of the half and hit workhorse White for a 6-yard score to lead 21-3.

Under pressure, Andrew Luck threw a poor pass that Patrick Chung intercepted at midfield, and Stephen Gostkowski made a 45-yard field goal for a 24-3 halftime lead.

"We're not going to win consistently until we learn how to get out of our own way," Luck said.

After Matthias Farley's interception of a pass bobbled by Chris Hogan, Indy could do nothing. Rookie Jordan Wilkins had the ball stripped from his hands by Devin McCourty four plays later.

But a second pick of Brady that was not his fault -- Rob Gronkowski had the ball

stolen and Najee Goode wound up with it -- helped the Colts get back into it for a short time.

Looking like vintage Luck, he brought his team 80 yards, including a pair of big third-down throws to Ebron, and Eric Swoope caught a 13-yard scoring pass to make it 24-17.

That's when everyone saw vintage Brady as he hit the half-century mark for TD throws by connecting with newcomer Gordon for 34 yards, the 71st player to catch a touchdown pass from Brady, an NFL mark.

"A great play Josh made jumping over two defenders," Brady said. "It tells you the kind of confidence I have in him in a short period of time. Obviously, he has earned it."

ABOVE: Colts kicker Adam Vinatieri, left, and Tom Brady speak at midfield after the game.
STEVEN SENNE / AP PHOTO

OPPOSITE ABOVE: Brady, left, throws a touchdown pass to Josh Gordon, under pressure from Colts defensive tackle Al Woods (99).
CHARLES KRUPA / AP PHOTO

OPPOSITE BELOW: Julian Edelman breaks away from Colts cornerback Chris Milton for extra yardage during the second half.
CHARLES KRUPA / AP PHOTO

BOX SCORE

	1	2	3	4	T
INDIANAPOLIS	0	3	7	14	24
NEW ENGLAND	7	17	0	14	38

Brady third in history to throw 500 TD passes

New England Patriots quarterback Tom Brady became the third player in NFL history to throw 500 touchdown passes, reaching the mark in the fourth quarter of Thursday night's game against the Indianapolis Colts.

Brady connected with wide receiver Josh Gordon on a 39-yard pass with 9:19 left to join Peyton Manning (539) and Brett Favre (508) as the only quarterbacks to throw for 500 touchdowns.

"Things like that, milestones and so forth, there's so many people who contribute," Brady said after the team's 38-24 victory. "I just think of all the people who have really worked hard. A quarterback doesn't throw them to himself. He needs people to catch, and block, and the defense to make plays, and coaches to coach. These are all great team awards. Pretty cool."

In joining that exclusive club, Brady became the first player to do so while playing for only one team.

"It's tremendous. It's a lot of touchdown passes to a lot of different guys, too. ... No quarterback I'd rather have than Tom Brady," coach Bill Belichick said.

Of Brady's 500 touchdown passes, here are a few notable highlights:

- His first touchdown pass was to wide receiver Terry Glenn on Oct. 14, 2001.

- He is one of two players to throw for 50 touchdowns in a season, along with Manning.

- His longest touchdown pass was 99 yards to Wes Welker, on Sept. 12, 2011, against Miami. There have been only 13 pass plays of 99 yards in league history.

- He has thrown 76 touchdown passes to tight end Rob Gronkowski, his most to any player. Randy Moss, with 39, is next on the list.

- He has thrown 68 touchdown passes against the Bills, his highest total against any team.

A wild win

Pats hold off Kansas City rally

Tom Brady needed everything he had to fend off Patrick Mahomes -- including his legs.

Stephen Gostkowski hit a 28-yard field goal as time expired, and the New England Patriots beat the Kansas City Chiefs 43-40 on Sunday night after blowing a big halftime lead.

Brady passed for 340 yards and a touchdown and ran for another score, diving head-first between two defenders in a rare run by the 41-year-old quarterback.

"I got close to the goal line and I just figured I'd try to get it in," Brady said of his late TD plunge. "We needed it."

New England's third straight win was Brady's 200th victory as a starting QB, tops all-time. He also passed former teammate Adam Vinatieri for most career wins in the regular season and playoffs combined with 227.

Brady got some help from rookie Sony Michel, who rushed 24 times for 106 yards and two touchdowns in another solid performance.

"It's tough to slow those guys down, they've been scoring a lot of points all year," Brady said. "They're gonna be pretty tough to stop. Glad we had our last shot and glad we took advantage of it."

It was the first loss of the season for the Chiefs (5-1), who were again let down by a defense that came in allowing an NFL-worst 462 yards per game.

New England (4-2) led 24-9 at intermission, but Mahomes directed

OCT. 14, 2018

PATRIOTS 43 CHIEFS 40

FOXBORO, MA GILLETTE STADIUM

OPPOSITE: Josh Gordon reaches for a pass as he is interfered with by a Chiefs defensive back during the first half.

MICHAEL DWYER / AP PHOTO

BELOW: Duron Harmon, left, prepares to intercept a pass in the end zone intended for Kansas City Chiefs tight end Travis Kelce, center rear, during the first half.

STEVEN SENNE / AP PHOTO

an impressive rally for Kansas City. He finished 23 of 36 for 352 yards in his first loss as a starting quarterback, with three of his four TD passes going to Tyreek Hill.

Mahomes threw two interceptions in the first half but was unflappable down the stretch. He found Hill for a 1-yard TD pass that made it 33-30 Kansas City with 8:38 left. With the Chiefs trailing 40-33, he connected with Hill again for a 75-yard score that tied the game with just over three minutes remaining.

"The last two weeks it seems like we just can't punch it in there and I feel like the second half we finally started getting it in the end zone," Mahomes said.

Brady used a 16-yard pass to James White and a 39-yard completion to Rob Gronkowski to get New England into field-goal range.

After electrifying the NFL during the first five weeks of the season with his freewheeling style and big arm, Mahomes looked unsure of himself early on.

He was able to complete some long passes to get the Chiefs into the red zone. But he turned the ball over twice in the first half and the high-scoring Chiefs were held to three field goals.

Everything changed in the second half.

First, Mahomes broke through with a 67-yard touchdown pass to Kareem Hunt . That was followed by a 14-yard TD strike to Hill that came on the heels of a fumble by Brady, helping trim New England's lead to 27-26 entering the fourth quarter.

A 39-yard field goal by Gostkowski stretched New England's lead to 30-26.

But Kansas City kept coming.

Tremon Smith took the ensuing kickoff 97 yards down the sideline to the Patriots 3, setting up Hill's go-ahead TD.

The Patriots responded, using 42-yard pass from Brady to Chris Hogan to help set up a 4-yard touchdown run by Brady that put the Patriots back in front.

Then, after forcing Kansas City into the first punt by either team on the night, Brady got the Patriots some breathing room when he hit Gronkowski for a 42-yard gain. The play set up 50-yard field goal by Gostkowski.

"We knew it was going to be a shootout," Hogan said. "We knew it could come down to fourth quarter football, and it came down to the last play."

OPPOSITE: Chiefs quarterback Patrick Mahomes passes under intense pressure from Patriots linebacker Dont'a Hightower (54) and defensive lineman Trey Flowers (98).
JIM MAHONEY / AP PHOTO

ABOVE: Rob Gronkowski gives a stiff arm to Chiefs free safety Ron Parker after catching a pass during the second half.
STEVEN SENNE/ AP PHOTO

BOX SCORE

	1	2	3	4	T
KANSAS CITY	6	3	17	14	40
NEW ENGLAND	10	14	3	16	43

Unanswered prayer

Bears Hail Mary on final play comes up just short

OCT. 21, 2018

PATRIOTS 38 BEARS 31

CHICAGO, IL SOLDIER FIELD

Tom Brady held his breath as he watched the final play unfold from the sideline.

He saw Mitchell Trubisky heave the ball toward the goal line, Kevin White haul it in and a swarming defense keep the ball out of the end zone. That was just enough to preserve another victory for New England.

Brady threw for three touchdowns and the Patriots hung on to beat the Chicago Bears 38-31 Sunday when White got stopped at the 1 on a 54-yard pass from Trubisky.

About four or five defenders swarmed White after he leaped to haul in that long heave and spun toward the goal line. Some Bears players tried to push him across. But he got stopped just short of the goal line, sealing the fourth straight win for New England.

"You hold your breath when I saw him jump up and catch it," Brady said. "I didn't have the angle on the goal line. He was getting close to the end zone. They were pushing and we were pushing. It was probably a half yard or a yard, pretty close. Good for us to hold them out."

Even if the execution wasn't perfect.

"Just too many people around the ball," said Josh Gordon, who was in on the play. "I went up to grab it. Somebody else went up to grab it. There was pushing and pulling, everything like that. He ended up with it so it was a great play... fortunately enough, we were able to hold him out of the end zone."

As for White?

"Just tried to fight and get in," he said. "Tried to change the game, make a big-time play. After I caught it, I thought I had a chance, like I said, for a split-second and once I felt a bunch of guys on me I knew it was over."

The Patriots (5-2) also got two special team's touchdowns and came out on top even though they were without Rob Gronkowski.

The five-time Pro Bowl tight end missed the game because of ankle and back injuries. But New England squeezed past the Bears (3-3).

Brady improved to 5-0 against Chicago, one of five teams yet to beat him. He was 25 of 36 for 277 yards and an interception.

Cordarrelle Patterson ran a kickoff back 95 yards for his sixth career return TD. Perhaps the play of the day was Dont'a Hightower's blocked

OPPOSITE: Patriots Josh Gordon (10), Jason McCourty (30) and Devin McCourty (32) leap and defend as Bears wide receiver Kevin White (11) jumps and catches a 54-yard Hail Mary pass at the New England Patriots one-yard line as time expires.
PAUL SPINELLI / AP PHOTO

BELOW: Chicago Bears receiver Kevin White, center, fights to reach the goal line as the Patriots defenders work to bring him down.
DAVID BANKS / AP PHOTO

ABOVE: Cordarrelle Patterson sprints for the endzone on a 95-yard kickoff return for a touchdown during the second quarter.
NAM Y. HUH / AP PHOTO

RIGHT: Kyle Van Noy recovers a blocked punt by Dont'a Hightower's and returns it 29-yards for a touchdown.
DAVID BANKS / AP PHOTO

OPPOSITE: Trey Flowers ducks under a block as he eyeballs Bears quarterback Mitchell Trubisky dropping back to pass.
PAUL SPINELLI / AP PHOTO

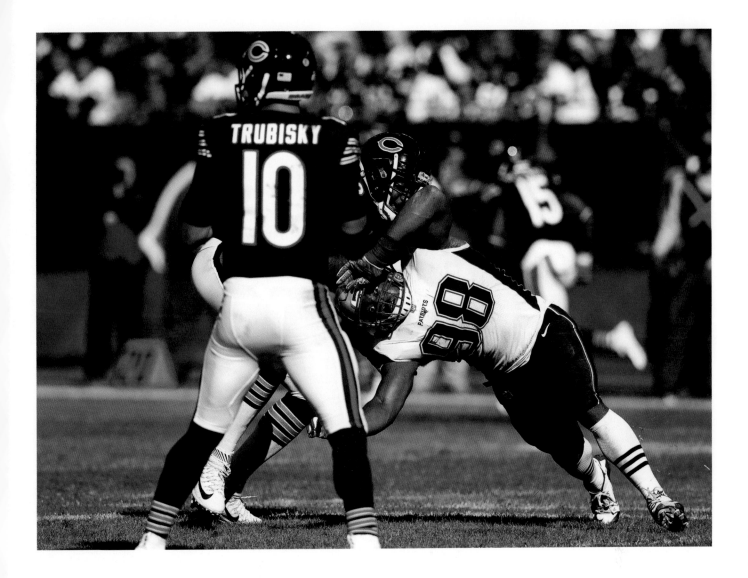

punt with 5:53 remaining the third quarter. Hightower blasted through the middle of the Chicago line and swatted the ball down with ease. Half the Patriots defense was in position to scoop it up, and Kyle Van Noy finally secured it and raced 29 for a touchdown that broke a 24-24 tie.

Hightower steamrolled Bears tight end Ben Braunecker to make the play.

"I'm power, not a finesse guy," Hightower said. "When I'm in there, I'm trying to play strong and tough and physical. That's what it was."

Gordon caught four passes for 100 yards. He spun past a tackler on a 55-yarder early in the fourth that put the ball on the 1 and set up a 2-yard reception by James White to make it 38-24 with 8:40 left.

White had 57 yards receiving and two TDs. He also ran for a team-high 40 yards.

Although the defense struggled containing the mobile Trubisky, safety Duron Harmon is encouraged by the 14 turnovers they've generated through seven games.

"Opportunities are going to come, and that's something we're excited about," Harmon said. "We're moving at a lot better pace than we have been the last few years."

BOX SCORE

	1	2	3	4	T
NEW ENGLAND	7	14	10	7	38
CHICAGO	10	7	7	7	31

Battle in Buffalo

McCourty's pick-6 seals the deal

Devin McCourty returned an interception 84 yards for a touchdown, and the New England Patriots' defense smothered the Buffalo Bills' anemic offense in a 25-6 win on Monday night.

James White scored on a 1-yard run, and the Patriots relied more on Stephen Gostkowski's leg than on Tom Brady's arm for their fifth straight win, which improved their AFC East-leading record to 6-2. Brady finished 29 of 45 for 324 yards, but was held without a touchdown pass for the first time this season.

Gostkowski hit four of five field-goal attempts, including two from 25 yards after New England drives stalled inside Buffalo's 10.

"They made it tough on us," Brady said. "We couldn't get anything going in the red zone, not enough positive plays down there. I think if we score those touchdowns, we feel a lot better. But they've been playing well all year, and they haven't given up many yards. We hung in there, grinded it out."

McCourty sealed the win with 5:54 remaining by intercepting Derek Anderson's pass over the middle intended for Charles Clay and taking it to the end zone.

Two plays before the pick, Bills tight end Jason Croom's diving one-handed touchdown catch was negated following a video review. Replays clearly showed Croom never had possession in attempting to make the 25-yard catch, which would have made it a one-score game.

McCourty's interception also came

OCT. 29, 2018

PATRIOTS 25
BILLS 6

BUFFALO, NY
NEW ERA FIELD

ABOVE: Buffalo Bills quarterback Derek Anderson, right, fumbles the ball as he's hit by linebacker Kyle Van Noy during the second half.
JEFFREY T. BARNES / AP PHOTO

OPPOSITE: Devin McCourty returns a fourth quarter interception 84-yards for a touchdown.
AARON M. SPRECHER / AP PHOTO

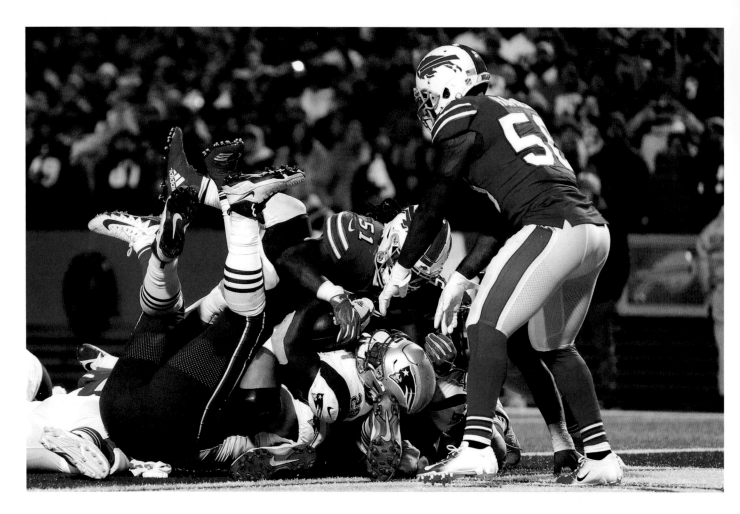

ABOVE: James White (28) falls back into the endzone for a 1-yard touchdown run.
JEFFREY T. BARNES / AP PHOTO

RIGHT: Stephen Gostkowski, with Ryan Allen holding, kicks one of his four field goals on the day.
ADRIAN KRAUS / AP PHOTO

OPPOSITE: Rob Gronkowski, right, makes an incredible catch against Bills defensive back Phillip Gaines during the second half.
JEFFREY T. BARNES / AP PHOTO

after White scored to cap a 10-play, 85-yard drive to put New England ahead 18-6 with 9:58 remaining.

"I felt like once our offense got one in the end zone, it was big for us to go out there and try to get a stop," McCourty said. "And it ended up being a turnover for a touchdown."

So much for the idea McCourty has slowed down at age 31.

"I'm not really worried about me losing a step," McCourty said. "I just go out there and play. Today I got to showcase a little bit of the speed. Hopefully, at 31, I can hold on to my speed a little bit longer."

Buffalo lost its third straight and dropped to 2-6 for its worst start since opening the 2010 season with eight losses.

Credit the Bills' defense for not playing the role of the expected pushover against a Brady-led offense that had scored 38 or more points in each of its past four games.

"You come out and you hold those guys to one touchdown and still can't get a win. It's tough, man," Bills cornerback Tre'Davious White said.

Buffalo's problem continued to be an offense that has managed just 87 points this season, and was held to under seven points for the fourth time. Stephen Hauschka accounted for the scoring by hitting field goals from 51 and 47 yards.

"It's clearly not good enough," coach Sean McDermott said of his sputtering offense. "I thought the defense came out and played well at times. Offensively, we shot ourselves in the foot a little bit there, and just couldn't get it going enough."

Anderson was escorted off the field with 1:25 left when he was sacked by Kyle Van Noy. Anderson was making his second start in place of rookie Josh Allen, who's listed as week to week with a sprained elbow on his throwing arm.

Anderson finished 22 of 39 for 290 yards and two interceptions.

Brady continued his string of career-long dominance over the Bills by improving to 29-3, extending the NFL record for most wins by a quarterback against one opponent.

The Patriots beat Buffalo for the seventh straight time and improved to 32-5 in their last 37 meetings under coach Bill Belichick.

BOX SCORE

	1	2	3	4	T
NEW ENGLAND	3	6	3	13	25
BUFFALO	0	3	3	0	6

Pats sack the Pack

Brady outduels Rodgers in 31-17 win

Tom Brady and Aaron Rodgers spent the week telling anyone who asked that the other guy was the better quarterback.

In the second matchup between the future Hall of Famers, it was the one with five Super Bowl rings who walked off the field with the victory.

Brady threw for 294 yards and a touchdown, and James White ran for two scores to lead the New England Patriots to a 31-17 victory over Rodgers and the Green Bay Packers on Sunday night. It was the sixth straight victory for the Patriots (7-2).

"We made some plays in the fourth quarter when we needed to," Brady said. "Anytime you beat a good football team it feels good. So, 7-2 is a long way from 1-2 where we were."

Rodgers completed 24 of 43 passes and two touchdowns but failed to rally his team after tying the game in the third quarter. Rodgers won the first matchup with Brady at Lambeau Field in 2014.

"If you play long enough, and you have the sustained greatness that Tom has had, there's going to be a lot of records," Rodgers said. "He's been the gold standard at quarterback for two decades."

It was 17-all late in the third quarter when Aaron Jones fumbled for Green Bay (3-4-1).

New England receiver Julian Edelman hit White on a 37-yard catch-and-run to set up White's second score, a 1-yard run. On the Patriots next possession, Brady connected with Josh Gordon for a 55-yard TD. Gordon caught five passes for 130 yards, the 12th 100-yard receiving game of his career.

With tight end Rob Gronkowski out with a back and ankle injury and

NOV. 4, 2018

**PATRIOTS 31
PACKERS 17**

FOXBORO, MA
GILLETTE STADIUM

OPPOSITE: Kyle Van Noy drills Green Bay Packers running back Aaron Jones during the second half.
STEVEN SENNE / AP PHOTO

BELOW: Josh Gordon breaks free for a 55-yard touchdown reception in the fourth quarter.
RYAN KANG / AP PHOTO

ABOVE: Packers quarterback Aaron Rodgers scrambles away from Patriots defensive tackle Adam Butler during the first half.
CHARLES KRUPA / AP PHOTO

RIGHT: Chris Hogan lets the home crowd know he just got a first down.
AARON M. SPRECHER / AP PHOTO

OPPOSITE: Two future Hall of Famers, Aaron Rodgers and Tom Brady, speak at midfield after the Patriots defeated the Packers.
STEVEN SENNE / AP PHOTO

leading rusher Sony Michel out for the second straight week with a knee issue, Brady and the Patriots had to get creative.

They again turned to receiver Cordarrelle Patterson to help carry the load in the backfield. Patterson was effective for the second straight week, rushing 11 times for 61 yards and a touchdown.

He worked in tandem with White to keep the Packers defense guessing. White took advantage and found space to turn short completions into first downs.

New England also capitalized on a pair of long flea-flicker passes to set up scores.

Rodgers was on target in the first half. He was elusive in the pocket and extended plays with his feet, keeping the Patriots' secondary off balance long enough to create space downfield or some big gains.

The longest was a 51-yard pass to Marquez Valdes-Scantling in the third quarter that helped set up Rodgers'

15-yard TD pass to Jimmy Graham that tied the game at 17. But the pocket got smaller in the second half as the Patriots defense sped him up, hitting him six times and sacking him once.

Brady completed 16 of his first 22 passes but had six straight incompletions in the third quarter.

There wasn't a turnover in the game until Green Bay's Jones was stripped by Lawrence Guy early in the fourth quarter. The fumble was recovered by Stephon Gilmore on the Patriots' 24.

New England quickly capitalized, using four straight completions by Brady and a 37-yard pass from Julian Edelman to get to the Packers' 2. White scored from a yard out two plays later to put the Patriots back in front 24-17.

"It was obviously a big play in the game," Packers coach Mike McCarthy said. "That was a turning point."

BOX SCORE

	1	2	3	4	T
GREEN BAY	3	7	7	0	17
NEW ENGLAND	7	10	0	14	31

The World Series champion Boston Red Sox are honored prior to the Green Bay game. Players and coaches ride onto the field in a duckboat as New England fans snapped photos.

STEVEN SENNE/ AP PHOTO

A Tennessee takedown
Pats no match for Titans

Nissan Stadium was rocking on Sunday, as the Tennessee Titans turned in a dominating performance against the New England Patriots.

For weeks, the Patriots have been struggling in the red zone, failing to convert short fields into touchdowns.

On Sunday, their troubles expanded to the entire field. New England's offense looked as lifeless as it's ever been in the Tom Brady-Bill Belichick era in a 34-10 loss to the Titans in Nashville.

Not that the defense helped matters, either, as Titans quarterback Marcus Mariota and the rest of Tennessee's offense had their way all day long.

The Titans scored on the game's first drive, with Mariota completing a 4-yard pass to Jonnu Smith to cap

off a ridiculously easy seven-play, 40-yard drive.

Stephen Gostkowski kicked a 52-yard field goal on New England's opening drive, only for Tennessee to march right back down field with a nine-play, 78-yard scoring drive which culminated in a Corey Davis 23-yard touchdown reception.

Davis was a monster for the Titans all game long, hauling in seven passes for 125 yards while routinely beating Stephon Gilmore in coverage.

James Develin had a 1-yard touchdown run to pull the Patriots within 17-10 early in the second quarter, but the Patriots would get no closer.

Tennessee made it a two-score game on a Derrick Henry 1-yard

NOV. 11, 2018

TITANS 34
PATRIOTS 10

NASHVILLE, TN
NISSAN STADIUM

OPPOSITE: Head coach Bill Belichick watches from the sidelines.
MARGARET BOWLES / AP PHOTO

BELOW: Tom Brady sits on the turf after being sacked in the second half.
MARK ZALESKI / AP PHOTO

touchdown run just before halftime, kicked a field goal in the third quarter, and put an end to any shot of a New England comeback with another Henry run in the fourth.

Things got so bad for the Patriots that Brian Hoyer replaced Brady midway through the fourth quarter with the outcome of the game long since decided.

"We didn't do much of anything well today, so everything was a problem," Patriots coach Bill Belichick said at his postgame news conference. "They were better than we were in that area (third downs), along with a lot of other ones. ... The Titans were clearly the better team and deserved to win. They did, soundly."

Brady completed 21 of his 41 passes for 254 yards, good enough for a passer rating of just 70.6 -- his second-lowest of the season following a similar debacle in Detroit.

Mariota, meanwhile, shined for the Titans. He was 16 for 24 for 228 yards and the two touchdown passes, and even added a catch for 21 yards.

The Patriots hardly targeted former cornerback Malcolm Butler, who started the game for his new team despite struggles in recent weeks. Dion Lewis, another former Patriot, was also relatively quiet with 57 rushing yards and just two catches for 11 yards.

Tennessee, of course, is coached by former New England linebacker Mike Vrabel, who spent eight seasons with the Patriots from 2001 to 2008.

Vrabel downplayed the significance of beating his former team. When asked about it, he said, "Look, I'm happy to get above .500. It's a good football team that we played and beat today."

ABOVE: Tennessee Titans wide receiver Corey Davis drops a pass in the end zone while covered by Patriots cornerback Jason McCourty.

AUSTIN ANTHONY / DAILY NEWS VIA AP PHOTO

OPPOSITE: James Develin scores the lone Patriots touchdown on the day on a 1-yard run during the second quarter.

PERRY KNOTTS / AP PHOTO

BOX SCORE

	1	2	3	4	T
NEW ENGLAND	3	7	0	0	10
TENNESSEE	17	7	3	7	34

A passing fancy

Brady sets records as Pats top Jets 27-13

NOV. 25, 2018

PATRIOTS 27 JETS 13

EAST RUTHERFORD, NJ
METLIFE STADIUM

Tom Brady set yet another NFL record. Ho-hum. The New England Patriots quarterback was more excited about earning another victory.

Brady threw two touchdown passes and became the career leader in total yards passing in regular-season and playoff games, leading the Patriots past the New York Jets 27-13 on Sunday.

"Just wins," Brady said. "That's what we're here for. I'm trying to be a part of as many of these as I can."

Well, the five-time Super Bowl champion certainly has lots of those.

The latest clinched the Patriots (8-3) their 18th straight season with a .500 record or better. That ranks second in NFL history to only Dallas, which had 21 in a row from 1965-85.

Brady had just one TD throw in his previous three games, but connected with Rob Gronkowski and Julian Edelman against the AFC East-rival Jets (3-8). The Patriots quarterback went 20 of 31 for 283 yards, giving him 79,416 for his career.

He also reached 3,000 yards passing for the 16th season, tying Peyton Manning for second in NFL history behind Brett Favre's 18.

That's all after missing Friday's practice with an illness after being limited during the week with a sore knee.

OPPOSITE: Rob Gronkowski, left, is congratulated by Julian Edelman after scoring on a 34-yard touchdown reception.
ADAM HUNGER / AP PHOTO

BELOW: Tom Brady looks to go deep downfield early in the second half.
SETH WENIG / AP PHOTO

ABOVE: Julian Edelman beats three Jets defenders on his way to a 21-yard touchdown reception.
BILL KOSTROUN / AP PHOTO

RIGHT: Rob Gronkowski battles Jets cornerback Morris Claiborne for the ball.
BILL KOSTROUN / AP PHOTO

OPPOSITE: New England Patriots fans let Tom Brady know he is the GOAT – greatest of all time.
BILL KOSTROUN / AP PHOTO

"I'd prefer to be healthy and practice all the time," Brady said. "That just wasn't the case."

He was plenty good enough.

Rookie Sony Michel ran for a season-best 133 yards and a TD , and the Patriots had 215 yards rushing -- responding well to coach Bill Belichick's challenge to his offense.

"We talked about being consistent week in and week out," Michel said, "playing Patriots football, being physical and run the ball and throw the ball and control the line of scrimmage."

Coming off a 34-10 loss to Tennessee two weeks ago, the Patriots avoided their second two-game losing streak of the season -- something the franchise hasn't experienced since 2015. New England, which improved to 3-3 on the road, has won five straight in the series against New York and eight of the past nine.

With Jets rookie Sam Darnold out with a foot strain, 39-year-old backup Josh McCown got his second straight start -- making this game the NFL's second-oldest QB combo at 80 years, 258 days with 41-year-old Brady going for New England. Only Carolina's Vinny Testaverde

(44) and Green Bay's Favre (38) in 2007 are an older combination at 82 years, 44 days old.

Brady got the better of McCown in this one, though, even though it took until late in the second half for the Patriots to pull away.

"We were not great in the red area, but we made enough plays," Brady said. "In every area, I think we can do a better job. We're certainly not where we want to be and we'll keep building for it. Hopefully, everyone can stay healthy."

Brady connected with Edelman for a 21-yard touchdown that put the Patriots ahead 20-13 with 1:52 left in the third quarter. The drive opened with a 27-yard reception by Chris Hogan, followed by a 27-yard run by James White. Brady found a wide-open Edelman, who ran through a tackle attempt by Jamal Adams and got into the end zone.

Michel added a 1-yard touchdown run with 8:54 left, one play after a video review reversed his TD run; his right knee was down before he reached the goal line. The score put the Patriots up 27-13 and sent many Jets fans streaming toward the exits.

BOX SCORE

	1	2	3	4	T
NEW ENGLAND	7	3	10	7	27
N.Y. JETS	7	3	3	0	13

Brady & Edelman

"He's always been kind of like my little brother, in a good way. I don't have a little brother, but he's kind of like a little brother and he knows how much I love him."
-Tom Brady

Teammates have called their relationship a "bromance." Patriots quarterback Tom Brady himself openly uses the word love to describe his bond with Julian Edelman, a receiver he's come to depend on during his career.

As the duo prepares to play in a fourth Super Bowl together, each says the connection might be tighter than ever — both on and off the field.

"We have a great relationship, Jules and I, and I trust him so much," Brady says. "He's always been kind of like my little brother, in a good way. I don't have a little brother, but he's kind of like a little brother and he knows how much I love him."

In Edelman's case, it's a little brother who has established himself as one of the best slot receivers in Patriots history.

He missed the entire 2017 season with a torn ACL and the first four games of this season for violating the league's performance enhancers policy. But the 32-year-old helped Brady steady an offense that struggled early this season and had to adjust following the suspension of Josh Gordon heading into the final two games.

Edelman ended the regular season with a team-high 850 receiving yards and was second on the team with 74 receptions and six touchdowns. His production has continued through New England's first two playoffs games, with Edelman hauling in 16 catches for a team-high 247 yards.

Heading into the matchup with the Rams, his 1,271 postseason receiving yards are the most in Patriots history. There are also just two receivers in NFL

postseason history with over 100 catches: Jerry Rice with 151 and Edelman with 105.

It's earned him high compliments not only from Brady, but from Rice, who praised Edelman as someone who has an attitude of "'I'm going to do what I want to do, and I'm going to go out and I'm going to ball."

It not unlike the determination used to describe Brady, who at age 41 continues to prove his skeptics wrong.

"He's a really good football player, the best," Edelman said. "He goes out and he consistently proves it. He's one of our leaders and he's a leader for a reason."

Though they first met as teammates in New England when Edelman was drafted by the Patriots a decade ago, he and Brady took remarkably similar paths to get to the NFL.

Both natives of California, each of them grew up idolizing the San Francisco 49ers' dynasty led by Joe Montana and Rice.

Brady played his college ball at Michigan, with Edelman eventually choosing Kent State across the border in Ohio.

Their stories continued to mirror each other when it came time for the NFL draft.

Brady infamously wasn't selected until the sixth round in 2000. Edelman, an undersized quarterback who

Chasing the NFL was a leap of faith for Edelman, who nearly signed a contract with the CFL's British Columbia Lions to play quarterback.

"I sat down with my father and basically, he's like 'Let's do it,'" Edelman recalled. "I just had an eerie feeling in my stomach and I told him I didn't grow up wanting to play in the CFL. I went and tried to play in the NFL. That was my decision. Everything happens for a reason."

Edelman was already a fan of Brady's when he arrived as a rookie, but he said he almost instantly recognized an underdog spirit in his new quarterback as well. As their relationship has evolved, they say they've developed their own sort of silent language on the field, and have unique ways to hype up each other.

An example was during the AFC championship game when video captured Edelman in Brady's face yelling, "You're too old!" as Brady sat on the bench after throwing a first-half touchdown pass.

Brady said he continues to be amazed by Edelman.

"Look at his stature. He wasn't built like Megatron (Calvin Johnson). He's just built the way he was built and I think he's just worked so hard over the years to learn how to play receiver," Brady said. "He's just done an incredible job."

Belichick wins 250th game

Pats roll over Vikings 24-10

The Patriots have thrived in the final month of the season since Bill Belichick and Tom Brady's arrival.

They're hoping their 24-10 victory over the Vikings is the start of another memorable December.

Tom Brady passed for 311 yards and a touchdown, Bill Belichick earned his 250th victory, including playoffs, as Patriots coach in Sunday's victory over Minnesota.

Including his 37 regular-season and postseason wins with the Browns, Belichick has 287 wins overall.

Brady completed 24 of 32 passes and has 579 touchdown passes, including the playoffs, tying him with Peyton Manning for the most all time.

James Develin added a career-high two touchdown runs as New England finished with 471 total yards. Brady said the diversity of their attack was his biggest takeaway.

"Seven guys running, eight guys catching -- that makes it hard for them to defend us," he said. "Hopefully we can keep it going."

The Patriots (9-3) have won eight of nine since starting the season 1-2. Belichick improved to 65-13

DEC. 2, 2018

PATRIOTS 24 VIKINGS 10

FOXBORO, MA GILLETTE STADIUM

OPPOSITE: Lawrence Guy stands up Minnesota Vikings running back Latavius Murray.
ELISE AMENDOLA / AP PHOTO

BELOW: Head coach Bill Belichick wears special shoes as part of the My Cause My Cleats campaign during his 250th win as Patriots head coach.
ELISE AMENDOLA / AP PHOTO

in December. Brady is 59-11. Both marks are NFL records for the most wins during that month for a coach and player.

The Patriots have clinched their 18th straight winning season. It is the second-longest streak in NFL history. The record is held by the Cowboys at 20 seasons from 1966-85.

Minnesota (6-5-1) has lost two of its past three. The Vikings entered the game allowing the third-fewest rushing yards in the league (93.6 per game). But New England was able to spread them out, rushing for 160 yards.

Kirk Cousins kept Minnesota in the game early, before faltering down the stretch. He finished 32 of 44 for 201 yards and touchdown but had two late interceptions.

With New England leading 10-7 in the third quarter, Stephen Gostkowski missed a 48-yard field-goal attempt wide right at the 6:26 mark. It snapped a streak of 35 straight makes in the regular season of less than 50 yards, going back to October of last season.

The Vikings tied the game on the ensuing series with Dan Bailey's 39-yard field goal.

But the Patriots bounced back, needing just four plays for Brady to cap a 75-yard drive with a 24-yard touchdown pass to Josh Gordon that put the Patriots back in front 17-10.

Following Minnesota's punt, the Patriots picked up where they left off. This time they needed only six plays to set up a 2-yard TD run by Develin that made it 24-10.

The Vikings survived a challenge by Belichick of a spot on a fourth down rush by Latavius Murray on their next possession. Belichick's challenge led to a brief verbal exchange between him and receiver Adam Thielen. It included linebacker Kyle Van Noy coming to his coach's defense.

"Everybody's out there battling," Patriots safety Devin McCourty said.

"Sometimes football comes down to a yard. ... But Bill's fiery. We see it every day."

But facing a fourth-and-11 seven plays later, the Vikings turned it over on downs after Cousins' pass to Laquon Treadwell came up short.

Minnesota got the ball back quickly after Brady threw his first interception in five games to Eric Kendricks. But a pass into the end zone by Cousins was tipped by J.C. Jackson and intercepted by Duron Harmon .

"Every guy on the offense, they're hungry. You know, just like the defense. We're all hungry," Patriots receiver Cordarrelle Patterson said. "We all know our role and we embrace it."

ABOVE: James Develin dives into the end zone to put the Patriots up 24-10.
RIC TAPIA / AP PHOTO

OPPOSITE ABOVE: Duron Harmon celebrates after intercepting Vikings quarterback Kirk Cousins pass in the endzone.
WINSLOW TOWNSON / AP PHOTO FOR PANINI

OPPOSITE BELOW: Tom Brady signals first down.
WINSLOW TOWNSON / AP PHOTO FOR PANINI

BOX SCORE

	1	2	3	4	T
MINNESOTA	0	7	3	0	10
NEW ENGLAND	7	3	7	7	24

Miami Meltdown

Dolphins score on last play to stun Pats 34-33

The celebratory mob scene in the corner of the end zone broke out far from Ryan Tannehill, leaving him in the open field, running and screaming as he waved his arms. Since he couldn't find anyone to hug, he flopped to the grass on his back, the job done and the game won.

"I collapsed -- just the emotion of the whole thing," Tannehill said.

Sixteen seconds from defeat, Tannehill threw a short pass and then watched his teammates save the season with the "Drake Escape."

Kenyan Drake ran the last 52 yards as the Dolphins scored on a pass and double lateral on the final play Sunday to beat the New England Patriots 34-33.

"They just made one more play than we did," Patriots coach Bill Belichick said.

And what a play. The Patriots were on the verge of clinching their 10th consecutive AFC East title when the Dolphins lined up at their 31 after a kickoff return trailing 33-28.

"You knew he wasn't throwing the ball 75 yards to the end zone," said Patriots safety Duron Harmon. "We knew that. We knew it was going to be a lateral situation. If the ball was at the 35-yard line or the 40-yard line, maybe we would be thinking of a Hail Mary."

Tannehill threw a 14-yard pass to Kenny Stills, who lateraled to DeVante Parker, who quickly lateraled to Drake along the sideline. He cut toward the middle and found a seam, helped by a block from guard Ted Larsen at the 30.

Drake beat two Patriots to the corner of the end zone -- defensive back J.C. Jackson and tight end Rob Gronkowski, who was on the field as part of New England's prevent defense.

OPPOSITE: Rob Gronkowski goes up high and snags a pass for a big gain in the first half.
TOM DIPACE/ AP PHOTO

BELOW: Miami Dolphins players mob running back Kenyan Drake after he scored the winning touchdown on a kick return on the last play of the game. .
LOGAN BOWLES / AP PHOTO

"Drake runs a 4.3, and Gronk probably runs a 4.6 or 4.7, so you feel good about that matchup," Tannehill said.

The Dolphins call the play "Boise" because it was borrowed from the Boise State playbook, and they had been working on it all year.

"You rep it in practice over and over," receiver Kenny Stills said. "Sometimes it's like, `Why are we doing this?' And now we know why."

It brought to mind other NFL last-second stunners, including Roger Staubach's "Hail Mary", the "Miracle in the Meadowlands" and the "Immaculate Reception". The play was the longest from scrimmage to win a game with no time remaining in the fourth quarter since the 1970 merger.

A number of New England players were asked to explain the final play, but none of them offered much insight.

"We can talk about that play until we're blue in the face," McCourty said. "As a defense, we just have to get to the ball and get him down. To be in a game like this and have so much on the line, just disappointing."

"Football," said Patriots quarterback Tom Brady, "is a crazy game."

Brady threw for 358 yards and three scores, but the stunned Patriots (9-4) lost in Miami for the fifth time in their past six visits. The Dolphins (7-6) came from behind five times to help their slim wild-card chances.

The Patriots' Stephen Gostkowski missed an extra point for the first time in 38 tries this season early in the game, and also missed a 42-yard field goal try. But his 32-yarder to cap a 55-yard drive put the Patriots ahead 30-28 with 6:45 left.

Belichick opted to have Gostkowski kick a 22-yarder in the closing seconds rather than pin the Dolphins near their goal line. Instead, Miami returned the ensuing kickoff to the 31 -- and on the next play pulled off a miracle.

LEFT & INSET: Miami Dolphins running back Kenyan Drake outruns the Patriots defenders to the end zone for the game winning touchdown. Drake ended up with the ball after multiple laterals by his Miami teammates.
LOGAN BOWLES & DAVID SANTIAGO / AP PHOTO

BOX SCORE

	1	2	3	4	T
NEW ENGLAND	6	21	0	6	33
MIAMI	7	14	7	6	34

New England Patriots center David Andrews (60)
lines up for the snap with fellow lineman Joe
Thuney (62) Trent Brown (77) and Shaq Mason (69)
at the line of scrimmage.

A long December
Road woes continue against Steelers

New England's struggles on the road continued in Pittsburgh on Sunday, costing them a chance to clinch a playoff spot for the second straight week.

Rookie running back Jaylen Samuels, making his second start in place of injured James Conner, ran for a career-high 142 yards and made a critical third-down reception in the fourth quarter as the Steelers snapped a three-game losing streak by holding off the Patriots 17-10.

"First off, give the Steelers credit. We lost to a good team today," Patriots head coach Bill Belichick said. "They played a little better than we did. We have to play better to win these games. Coach better. Play better. That's a good football team."

A victory would have given the Patriots their 10th straight AFC East title. While they still have two shots at it while finishing the regular season at home, the road issues don't appear to be going away. New England finished 3-5 away from Gillette Stadium, the first time the Patriots have a losing road record since 2009.

"We haven't played very well on the road," Brady said. "Obviously what we're doing isn't good enough."

The Steelers had dropped five straight to New England and only beaten Brady twice in his storied career. Despite never trailing, their third win over him wasn't assured

BELOW: Chris Hogan turns up field on his way to a 63-yard touchdown reception during the first quarter.
AARON M. SPRECHER / AP PHOTO

OPPOSITE: Duron Harmon (21) celebrates his second interception with teammate Malcom Brown.
RIC TAPIA / AP PHOTO

until Morgan Burnett knocked down Brady's heave to the end zone intended for Julian Edelman with 20 seconds to go.

"It's a big win for us," Roethlisberger said. "It's that time of year. We needed to win this football game."

Brady finished 25 of 36 for 279 yards with a touchdown and an interception. Pittsburgh held tight end Rob Gronkowski to two receptions for 21 yards. Brady flung a jump ball to Gronkowski deep in Pittsburgh territory midway through the fourth quarter that was picked off by cornerback Joe Haden, just Brady's fifth pick in 14 games against the Steelers.

"I was just trying to flick it out of bounds," Brady said. "Didn't want to take a sack. It shouldn't have happened."

The uncharacteristically sloppy Patriots were flagged 14 times for 106 yards, including a handful of offensive holding calls that blunted momentum. The Patriots had a second-and-5 at the Pittsburgh 11 with 37 seconds to go when right guard Shaq Mason was hit with a holding penalty that pushed the ball back to the Pittsburgh 21. The Patriots would get no closer.

"There's holding on every play in the NFL," Brady said. "It's what we do, we hold. ... If they're calling it, we've got to do a little bit less of it."

New England scored their lone touchdown when the Steelers left Chris Hogan wide open after biting on a reverse, leading to an easy 63-yard strike from Brady to the receiver.

"We've always won as a team and we lose as a team. When you lose close games there are a lot of plays you wish were different," Brady said after the loss. "I'm not going to make any excuses. We just have to do a better job."

ABOVE: Pittsburgh Steelers running back Jaylen Samuels carries the ball as Patriots free safety Devin McCourty (32) and cornerback Jason McCourty (right) make the tackle.
AARON M. SPRECHER / AP PHOTO

OPPOSITE: Pittsburgh Steelers cornerback Joe Haden soars high to intercepts a pass that quarterback Tom Brady was trying to throw away late in the second half.
KEITH SRAKOCIC/ AP PHOTO

BOX SCORE

	1	2	3	4	T
NEW ENGLAND	7	0	3	0	10
PITTSBURGH	7	7	0	3	17

Back on track

Pats earn 10th straight AFC East title

It's not every day that a team finds itself cheering for the one that beat it the season before in the Super Bowl.

This isn't the typical season for the New England Patriots.

Patriots players erupted in a loud cheer in the locker room as Eagles kicker Jake Elliott's 35-yard field goal sailed through the uprights as time expired to give Philadelphia a victory over the Houston Texans on Sunday.

Combined with the Patriots' 24-12 win over the Buffalo Bills just minutes before to snap a two-game losing streak, New England moved back into the No. 2 spot in the AFC with one game to play. A Patriots win over the Jets next week would give New England a first-round bye in the playoffs.

"Fly, Eagles, Fly!" receiver Julian Edelman said afterward.

It was a perfect ending to a less than perfect day for the Patriots.

New England (10-5) earned their 10th straight AFC East title with Sony Michel running for 116 yards and a touchdown. It also improved to 7-0 at home this season and became the first franchise in NFL history to earn playoff berths in 10 straight seasons.

Tom Brady went 13 of 24 for 126 yards, a touchdown and two interceptions -- his lowest output since he passed for 123 yards in a 2003 loss to the Bills.

"We didn't have our best day in the passing game. But it felt good to win. At this time of year, whatever it takes to win, that's what you've got to do,"

DEC. 23, 2018

PATRIOTS 24
BILLS 12

FOXBORO, MA
GILLETTE STADIUM

OPPOSITE: J..C. Jackson intercepts a pass intended for Buffalo Bills wide receiver Deonte Thompson.
ELISE AMENDOLA / AP PHOTO

BELOW: James White dives for the pylon to score a touchdown as Bills safety Micah Hyde defends..
STEVEN SENNE / AP PHOTO

ABOVE: Julian Edelman runs away from Bills defenders Corey Thompson, left, Lorenzo Alexander and Micah Hyde, right, on his way to a 32-yard third quarter touchdown reception.
ELISE AMENDOLA / AP PHOTO

RIGHT: Edelman, right, rolls over Bills defenders including Rafael Bush (20). Edelman never touched the ground and proceeded to score on the play.
STEVEN SENNE / AP PHOTO

OPPOSITE: Buffalo Bills quarterback Josh Allen tries to flip the ball to a receiver as Patriots defenders Trey Flowers, left, and Lawrence Guy chase him down.
ELISE AMENDOLA / AP PHOTO

Brady said. "And we still have one hugely important game left. We have to finish strong."

It was Michel's fourth 100-yard rushing game of the season.

It helped mask Brady's mild day. The two interceptions were his third time with multiple picks in a game this season. He now has 11 interceptions in 2018, his most since 2013.

Brady's touchdown pass of the game came thanks to a heads-up play by Julian Edelman in the third quarter.

Leading 14-6 and facing fourth-and-4 on the Bills 32, Brady found Edelman over the middle on a quick slant. Edelman was tackled and rolled up by safety Rafael Bush, but Edelman never touched the ground. He got up and sprinted into the end zone.

Brady's interceptions were among three turnovers by the Patriots on the day, but Buffalo was only able to turn them into three points. Leading 24-6 in fourth quarter, he was replaced by backup Brian Hoyer.

Asked why he pulled Brady with more than six minutes to play, coach Bill Belichick said because "I thought it was the right thing to do."

Rookie quarterback Josh Allen was bottled up for most of the day, limited to 20 of 41 for 217 yards with two interceptions. He ran five times for 30 yards. Buffalo finished with 72 rushing yards, the first time in five games it failed to rush for 100 or more.

"Gotta get better," Allen said. "We'll learn from this one. New England is the team that teams want to be. The trajectory of where we want to put this team and how they can sustain success, so yeah we're gonna learn from this one."

After going three plays and out on their first drive of the day, the Patriots went to the run game to score the game's first touchdown. New England ran six straight times, capped by a 4-yard TD run by Michel. It was Michel's first touchdown since New England's Week 12 win over the Jets.

Following a Buffalo punt, the Patriots crossed into Bills' territory again, but gave the ball back when Rex Burkhead fumbled. But Stephen Hauschka's 43-yard field goal attempt hit the crossbar.

After both teams exchanged punts, New England pushed its lead to 14-0 in the second quarter via a 27-yard touchdown run by James White.

BOX SCORE

	1	2	3	4	T
BUFFALO	0	0	6	6	12
NEW ENGLAND	7	7	7	3	24

Jets grounded 38-3

Pats secure 1st-round playoff bye

DEC. 30, 2018

PATRIOTS 38 JETS 3

FOXBORO, MA GILLETTE STADIUM

It is rare that you get two wins in one game but that is exactly what happened to the New England Patriots.

Tom Brady threw for three first-half touchdowns and New England clinched its ninth straight first-round bye in the playoffs on Sunday with a 38-3 victory over the New York Jets. The Patriots (11-5) finished the season undefeated at home, where they'll have at least one playoff game.

"Essentially, we won next week because we won today," coach Bill Belichick said. "We'll see who our next opponent is, but we know they'll be good or they wouldn't be playing this time of the year."

After back-to-back December losses left the Patriots with a losing record on the road, they finished with two straight wins in New England to finish with the NFL's only perfect home record and avoid playing in the wild-card round for the first time since 2009.

The Patriots could have still earned the No. 1 seed in the AFC with losses by both Kansas City and the Los Angeles Chargers on the last day of the regular season. But the Chiefs beat the Raiders 35-3, locking New England into the second seed.

"Eleven and five is nothing to be sad about," Brady said. "We fought pretty hard and put ourselves in good position."

Jets rookie Sam Darnold, who had

LEFT: Adam Butler, right, forces a fumble by New York Jets quarterback Sam Darnold.
CHARLES KRUPA / AP PHOTO

OPPOSITE: Rex Burkhead tries to escape the grasp of New York Jets nose tackle Steve McLendon.
STEVEN SENNE/ AP PHOTO

Kyle Van Noy sprints for the end zone after recovering a fumble by New York Jets quarterback Sam Darnold. Van Noy scored on the play.

CHARLES KRUPA / AP PHOTO

been playing well since returning from a foot injury, completed 16 of 28 passes for 167 yards, but he also had a fumble that gave New England a touchdown . In what turned out to be the final game for Jets coach Todd Bowles, New York (4-12) lost for the ninth time in 10 games.

"I'm not going to talk about my job. That's been consistent since I've been here," said Bowles, who won 10 games in his first season but just 14 in the next three combined.

The Jets announced Bowles' firing a few hours after the game.

Brady completed 24 of 33 passes for 250 yards and four scores overall, bouncing back from his worst performance since 2006 -- a 48.3 passer rating in a 24-12 win over Buffalo. That, combined with the team's losses in Miami and Pittsburgh, again raised doubts whether the 41-year-old quarterback of the five-time Super Bowl champions had reached the end of their run.

But now they're back where they usually are: AFC East champions, a first-round bye, and a team no one is eager to play in the postseason.

"No matter the situation, even when it's not looking good, everybody wants to ignore us and say we're finished," safety Duron Harmon said. "We just ignored the noise, come to fight, work hard, every week."

After punting on their first possession, the Patriots scored on three straight drives.

Brady hit James White for a 17-yard TD late in the first quarter, and then connected with Rex Burkhead early in the second. After Elijah McGuire fumbled on the Jets' first play of the second quarter, Devin McCourty picked it up and ran it 14 yards to the 8.

Five plays later, Brady scrambled right and found Phillip Dorsett in the back of the end zone to make it 21-3. New England opened a 28-3 lead in the third quarter when defensive lineman Adam Butler knocked the ball out of Darnold's arm as he raised it to throw; Kyle Van Noy picked it up and ran 46 yards for the score.

Julian Edelman added a 6-yard TD catch in the fourth.

ABOVE: Tom Brady, left, drops back to pass to wide receiver Chris Hogan, foreground, during the second half.
CHARLES KRUPA / DAILY NEWS VIA AP PHOTO

OPPOSITE: James White drags New York Jets defensive back Rontez Miles as he dives across the goal line for a touchdown during the first half.
STEVEN SENNE / AP PHOTO

BOX SCORE

	1	2	3	4	T
N.Y. JETS	3	0	0	0	3
NEW ENGLAND	7	14	7	10	38

WORLD CHAMPIONS

The New England Patriots special teams unit stares down
Chargers linebacker Kyle Wilson prior to kickoff.

Kansas City bound

Michel scores 3 TDs as Patriots roll past Chargers 41-28

Sony Michel ran for 129 yards and had three touchdowns and the New England Patriots beat the Los Angeles Chargers 41-28 in the divisional playoffs on Sunday to earn their eighth straight trip to the AFC championship game.

New England (12-5) will play at Kansas City in next week's AFC title game. The Patriots beat the Chiefs 43-40 in Foxborough in Week 6.

It is the 13th conference championship game appearance by the Patriots during the Tom Brady-Bill Belichick era.

"It's going to be a good game," Brady said of the rematch with the Chiefs. "They're a good team. We played them earlier this year. I know everybody thinks we suck and, you know, we can't win any games, so we'll see. It'll be fun."

Quarterback Philip Rivers finished 25 of 51 for 331 yards, three touchdowns and an interception. He is 0-5 in games played in Foxborough, including 0-3 in the postseason. The Chargers (13-5) haven't reached the AFC title game since the 2007 season.

Brady finished 34 of 44 for 343 yards and a touchdown. James White tied Darren Sproles' NFL postseason record with 15 catches totaling 97 yards while Julian Edelman had nine catches for 151 yards.

After winning the coin toss, the Patriots chose to receive, rather than defer their choice to the second half.

JAN. 13, 2019

PATRIOTS 41
CHARGERS 28

FOXBORO, MA
GILLETTE STADIUM

AFC DIVISIONAL

OPPOSITE: Rex Burkhead gets a lift from Rob Gronkowski, center, as Tom Brady joins the celebration after Burkhead's touchdown.
CHARLES KRUPA / AP PHOTO

BELOW: Sony Michel bursts up the middle for a 14-yard touchdown run.
MARGARET BOWLES/ AP PHOTO

James White dances away from the San Diego defense. White tied Darren Sproles' NFL postseason record with 15 catches in the game.

AARON M. SPRECHER / AP PHOTO

Perhaps this was head coach Bill Belichick's way of sending a message to his troops as New England scored on its first four possessions of the game to build a 35-7 halftime lead.

"I think it was," center/ co-captain David Andrews stated. "We went out there and started fast. That's what we wanted to do and were able to do it today. Those first few drives we played really well, exactly how we wanted to. When things are clicking like that, it's a hard thing to stop."

The Chargers added three touchdowns in the second half, but it was much too late.

"We dug ourselves a hole in the first half," Chargers coach Anthony Lynn said. "One game doesn't define where we are as a football team."

Rivers seemed poised to keep Los Angeles in the game, connecting with Keenan Allen for a 43-yard score on Los Angeles' first offensive possession. It was the longest touchdown of Allen's career, including the postseason.

RIGHT: Rob Gronkowski fights off Chargers cornerback Michael Davis as he gains yards after the catch.
MARGARET BOWLES / AP PHOTO

OPPOSITE: Julian Edelman and Chargers linebacker Uchenna Nwosu collide helmet-to-helmet during the second half.
CHARLES KRUPA / AP PHOTO

It turned out to be just a blip. The Chargers punted the four other times they had the ball in the first half.

"We understood we had to not let [Rivers] be comfortable in the pocket, not allow him to step up [and throw], because he's a great quarterback," observed defensive end Trey Flowers. "We had to pressure him and I think we executed that well today. We had to bring our A-game and I think we did."

The Patriots were efficient throughout the opening 30 minutes, going 5 for 5 in the red zone, 5 of 6 on third down and committing only one penalty.

New England didn't go three-and-out for the first time until its fifth offensive touch of the day when it punted with 3:32 left in the second quarter.

But Ryan Allen's 48-yard punt was fumbled by Desmond King, sending the ball rolling toward the sideline. The referees ruled the ball went out of bounds before New England's Albert McClellan appeared to recover it. But the play was reversed after a challenge by Bill Belichick.

The turnover proved costly, with the Patriots scoring just four plays later when Michel crossed the goal line from 5 yards for his third touchdown of the half.

New England established the run early, creating big holes in a Chargers defense that ended the regular season ranked ninth in the NFL, allowing just 106 rushing yards per game.

Michel carried 16 times for 105 yards in the first half. He set the tone early, scoring from 1 yard on the opening possession of the game. It capped a 14-play, 83-yard drive in which he rushed five times for 15 yards and had a 9-yard reception.

The Patriots added scoring drives of 67, 58, 87 and 35 yards.

Now, if the Patriots want to advance to yet another Super Bowl – their third straight– they'll have to do something they've not done well this year: Win a game on the road.

"It'll be a tough game for us [at Kansas City], but we've got a lot of guys with a lot of character in this locker room," special teams co-captain Matthew Slater said. "We have a lot of belief, so, we'll see where that gets us."

BOX SCORE

	1	2	3	4	T
L.A. CHARGERS	7	0	7	14	28
NEW ENGLAND	14	21	3	3	41

Instant classic

Pats earn third straight Super Bowl appearance

The Patriots are headed back to the Super Bowl.

It took them overtime and more of Tom Brady's brilliance to get there -- for the third straight year. While the folks back home dealt with a frigid storm, Brady blew through Kansas City's exhausted defense on a 75-yard drive to Rex Burkhead's 2-yard touchdown run in a 37-31 victory Sunday for the AFC championship.

The drive, during which New England (13-5) had three third-down conversions, was reminiscent of when the Patriots beat Atlanta in the only Super Bowl to go to OT two years ago.

"Overtime, on the road against a great team," Brady said. "They had no quit. Neither did we. We played our best football at the end. I don't know, man, I'm tired. That was a hell of a game."

Awaiting them in Atlanta are the Los Angeles Rams, who won 26-23 in overtime in New Orleans for the NFC championship. The Rams (15-3) last made the Super Bowl in 2002 while based in St. Louis, losing to the Patriots.

New England benefited from two critical replay reviews and made its ninth Super Bowl with Brady at quarterback and Bill Belichick as coach.

Several times, the Patriots appeared to have it won, only to see Kansas City

JAN. 20, 2019

PATRIOTS 37 CHIEFS 31

KANSAS CITY, MO ARROWHEAD STADIUM

AFC CHAMPIONSHIP

OPPOSITE: Phillip Dorsett spikes the ball as he celebrates his 29-yard touchdown.
CHARLIE RIEDEL / AP PHOTO

BELOW: Tom Brady celebrates with his teammates.
CHARLIE NEIBERGALL / AP PHOTO

(13-5) come back in spectacular fashion.

Brady, at 41 already the oldest quarterback to have played in a Super Bowl, drove New England 65 yards in 1:24 for Burkhead's go-ahead 4-yard touchdown with 39 seconds left in regulation. That was enough time, though, for his far younger counterpart, the 23-year-old All-Pro Mahomes, to take the Chiefs 48 yards for a Harrison Butker 39-yard field goal with 8 seconds left to force overtime.

In the end, it was a flip of the coin that decided the AFC Championship because the Chiefs weren't stopping Tom Brady in overtime. Not a chance.

"I saw heads," said safety Devin McCourty, "and I knew what was gonna happen at the end of this one."

The Chiefs never saw the ball in overtime leaving many fans across the country calling for a change to the NFL rules.

"I thought if we got the chance," Mahomes said, "we'd score."

Mahomes finished 16 of 31 for 295 yards and three touchdowns.

An apparent muff by the usually reliable Julian Edelman on a fourth-quarter punt return was overturned by a lengthy video review, prompting raucous booing and some demonstrative arguing from the usually laid-back Andy Reid. Edelman definitely touched his next try when Brady's pass deflected off his hands directly to safety Daniel Sorensen. His 22-yard return set up Kansas City at the Patriots 23, and Damien Williams, who scored three times, had no defender near him down the left sideline for the score that made it 21-17, KC's first lead.

Back came Brady, engineering a 75-yard march on which Chris Hogan's diving one-handed catch on third down appeared to touch the ground. Reid challenged -- and lost.

ABOVE: Chris Hogan makes an incredible fourth quarter catch with Chiefs cornerback Steven Nelson playing tight defense on him. Kansas City challenged the pass completion ruling, but the catch was upheld.
CHARLIE NEIBERGALL / AP PHOTO

OPPOSITE: Trey Flowers celebrates after sacking Chiefs quarterback Patrick Mahomes during the first half.
ELISE AMENDOLA / AP PHOTO

Kansas City Chiefs quarterback Patrick Mahomes (15) eludes the rush of Patriots middle linebacker Kyle Van Noy (53) and teammate John Simon (55).

ABOVE: Rex Burkhead dives into the end zone for the game-winning touchdown.

ELISE AMENDOLA / AP PHOTO

RIGHT: Sony Michel takes a hard hit from Chiefs defensive back Eric Berry (29) and inside linebacker Anthony Hitchens (53).

CHARLIE RIEDEL / AP PHOTO

OPPOSITE: Head coach Bill Belichick, left, hands off the Lamar Hunt Trophy to quarterback Tom Brady, far right, after defeating the Kansas City Chiefs in the AFC Championship game.

CHARLIE RIEDEL / AP PHOTO

Minutes later, rookie Sony Michel scored from the 10, his second TD of the night.

With 3 1/2 minutes remaining, there was plenty of time for more points. Williams' 2-yard run gave the Chiefs a 28-24 edge that New England took up most of the remaining time overcoming. The Patriots were helped by an offside call on linebacker Dee Ford that negated an interception which would have clinched a KC victory.

"I couldn't be prouder to be on this team, how hard we fought, defense, offense, special teams, getting a victory on the road in the AFC Championship Game," said Patriots tight end Rob Gronkowski who came up with a key catch in overtime. "It was one of my sweeter victories, definitely, in my career."

On a night the defense shut out the Chiefs in the first half, limiting them to 32 yards, Brady needed to produce yet another big finish to counteract Patrick Mahomes, who awakened for his second 31-point second half of the season against the Patriots.

"You never want a game to come down to those situations, but you're always comfortable with Tom," Gronkowski said. "He's always prepared. He's always ready for his moments. That's why he's the greatest quarterback, hands down."

Gronk summed up the night with, "It was an awesome team win and it's just awesome to be going to the Super Bowl three years in a row."

BOX SCORE

	1	2	3	4	OT	T
NEW ENGLAND	7	7	3	14	6	37
KANSAS CITY	0	0	7	24	0	31

WORLD CHAMPIONS

Quarterback Tom Brady and tight end Rob Gronkowski, left, share a laugh in the locker room following the AFC Championship game.
ELISE AMENDOLA / AP PHOTO

Patriots and Rams
get settled in Atlanta as Super Bowl LIII approaches

Tom Brady and the New England Patriots have arrived. So have Jared Goff and the Los Angeles Rams.

Now it's time for them to get to work.

The teams landed in Atlanta on Sunday and will practice this week before squaring off in the NFL's main event, Super Bowl LIII, next Sunday.

The AFC champion Patriots hosted a rally at Gillette Stadium earlier in the day before heading to the airport and boarding their flight.

"We're not at the end yet," Brady told the fans in Foxborough, Massachusetts. "We've got one more to go."

It's New England's third straight Super Bowl trip and fourth in five years – and the ninth overall in the Brady-Bill Belichick era.

The Patriots, who beat the then-St. Louis Rams 20-17 for their first title in Super Bowl XXXVI after the 2001 season, are looking to hoist the Lombardi Trophy for the sixth time, which would tie the Pittsburgh Steelers for the most in the Super Bowl era.

The NFC champion Rams are back in the city where they won their only title after the 1999 season, when they beat Tennessee 23-16 in Super Bowl XXXIV.

Among those in the crowd to greet the team upon their arrival was Hall of Famer and former Rams defensive-end Jack Youngblood who played for the rams in the '70s and '80s. He told the team to "capture every moment that you possibly can because this one of the most special things that you do. One of the special moments in your lifetime."

During the team's pre-flight rally at the construction site where the Rams' multibillion-dollar stadium is rising in Inglewood, California, fans chanted "Greg! The! Leg!" for kicker Greg Zuerlein, who made a 57-yard field goal in overtime to beat New Orleans in the NFC title game.

Zuerlein strained his non-kicking foot at halftime of that game by slipping on a turf-covered metal plate during warmups on the Superdome field. The injury doesn't appear to be serious, and the Rams expect him to

kick in the Super Bowl, coach Sean McVay said.

Both teams are schedule to participate in media night activities later Monday, when the excesses of the Super Bowl buildup usually are on the most vivid display. From there the teams will make themselves at him in their respective hotels. The NFC champion Rams will be staying at the JW Marriott Atlanta Buckhead, a 371-room hotel connected to Lenox Square mall. The AFC champion Patriots will stay at the Hyatt Regency Atlanta hotel downtown.

The Rams are making their first appearance since losing the 2002 game that launched the Patriots dynasty. The previous time an L.A.-based Rams team was in the Super Bowl was after the 1979 season, where they lost to the Steelers.

If anyone had any question whether Tom Brady would consider retiring after the Super Bowl, win or lose, the iconic Patriots quarterback has apparently put it to rest.

"Zero," the 41-year-old Brady apparently replied when asked if there was any chance Super Bowl LIII would be his final NFL game.

LEFT: New England Patriots' Devin McCourty, front, and brother Jason McCourty arrive at the Hartsfield-Jackson Atlanta International Airport for Super Bowl LIII.
MATT ROURKE / AP PHOTO

Tale of the Tape

2018 REGULAR SEASON	NEW ENGLAND	LOS ANGELES RAMS
Record	11-5	13-3
Divisional Standings	1st	1st
Total Yards Gained	6,295	6,738
Total Offense (Rank)	393.4 (5)	421.1 (2)
Rush Offense	127.3 (5)	139.4 (3)
Pass Offense	266.1 (8)	281.7 (5)
Points Per Game	27.3 (4)	32.9 (2)
Touchdowns Scored	51	60
Third Down Conversion Pct.	40.8	45.0
Team Passer Rating	97.8	100.7
Total Yards Allowed	5,746	5,737
Total Defense (Rank)	359.1 (21)	358.6 (19)
Rush Defense	112.7 (11)	122.3 (23)
Pass Defense	246.4 (22)	236.3 (14)

2018 REGULAR SEASON	NEW ENGLAND	LOS ANGELES RAMS
Points Allowed/ Game	20.3 (7)	24.0 (20)
Touchdowns Allowed	36	44
Third Down Defense (Pct.)	38.6	37.2
Field Goals Made/ Attempted	27/32	34/41
Possession Avg.	31:05	30:42
Sacks Allowed/Yards Lost	21/147	33/223
Sacks Made/Yards	30/238	41/326
Passing TD/Int. (Off.)	29/11	32/12
Passing TD/Int. (Def.)	29/18	31/18
Penalties Against/ Yards	93/744	96/878
Punts/Avg.	64/45.1	43/46.3
Takeaway/Giveaway Ratio	+10 (5)	+11 (4)

The New England Patriots participate during the NFL's
Opening Night media event for Super Bowl 53.
DAVID GOLDMAN / AP PHOTO

Tom Brady and Rob Gronkowski play around with the fans.
DAVID J. PHILLIP / AP PHOTO

Camdyn Clancy has some fun with Julian Edelman during Opening Night.
DAVID J. PHILLIP / AP PHOTO

James White grins as he answers questions for the crowd.
JOHN BAZEMORE / AP PHOTO

Official Super Bowl LIII tickets.
Face value $950 per ticket.
DAVID J. PHILLIP / AP PHOTO

Goff vs Brady

Goff, 17 years Brady's junior, on equal ground at Super Bowl

Jared Goff was 7 years old when Tom Brady beat the Rams to win his first Super Bowl in early 2002. The kid has been a fan of the superstar ever since.

Goff is now 24, the same age as Brady was then. When Brady plays in his ninth Super Bowl in Atlanta for the New England Patriots, Goff will be on the other sideline for Los Angeles, neither star-struck nor cocky.

Their 17-year age gap is the biggest between starting quarterbacks in Super Bowl history. Yet the passing years apparently mean little to Brady, and they're just as unimportant to Goff, who sees no advantage in his youth and no disadvantage in his inexperience.

"It's a guy that I've looked up to for so long," Goff said. "Now I get a chance to play in a Super Bowl with him. We do respect him, but I'm going to go out there and do my best and be the best I can be, and hopefully come out with a win."

Brady, now 41, insists the years haven't changed him much from his first Super Sunday against the then-St. Louis Rams in 2002.

"In many ways, I'm similar," Brady said this week while preparing for the NFL's biggest stage. "I don't think in the end that things are that different for me. I loved playing then, I still love playing now."

Both quarterbacks will be under a relentless spotlight in the next week. Brady lives his life under that glare, while Goff is still getting used to it after just three years of being a No. 1 overall pick who stumbled early, but grew quickly into a successful quarterback.

Rams quarterback Jared Goff gets a chance to visit with Patriots quarterback Tom Brady during Opening Night in Atlanta.
JOHN BAZEMORE/ AP PHOTO

Goff doesn't admit to seeing this Super Bowl as a chance to step into Brady's echelon as one of the league's elite passers, even if that's what much of the football world is telling him. But after Goff led the Rams to 24 wins and two playoff victories over the past two years, the Rams already think he's there.

"We're very confident in his ability to lead us, knowing that it's a big game," Rams coach Sean McVay said. "I think Jared will be himself, which is exactly what we want him to be."

"Tom Brady is what playing quarterback is supposed to look like," McVay said. "He plays the position at a high level, with the decision making, the timing, the rhythm, the accuracy, the ownership of what they're trying to get done. I have so much respect for him. He's an elite competitor and it's going to be a great challenge trying to defend him."

Goff and Brady are from different generations, but the quarterbacks have a few things in common.

They're both from the Bay Area, with Brady growing up on the Peninsula and Goff in Marin County. Neither was a can't-miss NFL prospect heading into college, but neither let it stop him.

Already the winningest quarterback in NFL history, Brady will play in his 40th playoff game in Atlanta. Goff is playing in his fourth, but he is riding the momentum of his first two career postseason victories in the past two games.

The win over New Orleans wasn't his best performance of the season, but it was probably the most satisfying.

"What stood out was the way that he was able to weather the storm," McVay said. "The mental toughness was displayed by the team as a whole, and Jared kind of personified that with the way that he handled the game, his overall command, making big throws when we needed it the most. ... The competitive greatness showed up in a big way."

Goff and Brady have only faced each other once before. In December 2016, Brady became the NFL's career victories leader in a 26-10 victory at New England, while Goff threw two interceptions in his third career start.

Goff met Brady for the first time at that game. They're friendly, but not yet close

When asked if it feels surreal to be heading toward a Super Bowl showdown with the mighty Patriots and a quarterback who has been winning championships for his entire life, Goff stifled a grin.

"No," he replied. "I've played these guys before."

Quarterback Tom Brady speaks at midfield with Rams quarterback Jared Goff following the Patriots 26-10 win Dec. 4, 2016. It was Goff's first head-to-head match-up with the future Hall of Famer.
STEVEN SENNE/ AP PHOTO

Super Bowl Champions

The Brady-Belichick dynasty rolls on

Defenses dominated what was supposed to be a super shootout until Tom Brady led one classic drive to win the New England Patriots their record-tying sixth Super Bowl.

Brady threw two perfect passes to Rob Gronkowski to set up rookie Sony Michel's 2-yard score -- the only touchdown in the lowest-scoring Super Bowl ever. That put New England up 10-3. A late field goal clinched the win over the Rams 13-3.

In a season in which all sorts of offensive records were set, this Super Bowl rewrote the defensive record book.

"We were just grinding it out," Brady said. "We were able to put some things together. ... I just felt like we had to keep grinding it out all night. Finally got a touchdown and the defense played the best game of the year," Brady said.

No Super Bowl had gone into the fourth quarter without a touchdown. This one did, tied 3-3 -- even though these teams combined to average over 60 points a game.

When the Patriots needed a score, Brady, the oldest winning quarterback in a Super Bowl at 41, completed four straight passes, including a pair covering 47 yards to Gronkowski. The second, on which the star tight end beat two defenders, ended at the Los Angeles 2, the only time either team was inside the 20-yard line. Michel ran off left tackle for his sixth postseason touchdown.

"He knows to trust in me and throw that ball," Gronkowski said, "and I'm going to grab it."

FEB. 3, 2019

PATRIOTS 13
RAMS 3

ATLANTA, GA
MERCEDES-BENZ STADIUM

SUPER BOWL

OPPOSITE: Patriots defensive back Stephon Gilmore makes a huge fourth quarter interception on a pass intended for Los Angeles Rams receiver Brandin Cooks (12).
FRANK FRANKLIN II / AP PHOTO

BELOW: Patriots center David Andrews kisses the Lombardi Trophy after winning Super Bowl LIII.
CHARLIE RIEDEL/ AP PHOTO

Julian Edelman, the outstanding receiver who missed the 2017 season with a knee injury, was the game's MVP with 10 receptions for 141 yards.

With 4:17 left, All-Pro Stephon Gilmore picked off an ill-advised pass by Rams quarterback Jared Goff, who seemed overwhelmed by the big stage all night, at the New England 2.

Stephen Gostkowski made a 41-yard field goal with 1:12 remaining, completing a 72-yard march that took more than three minutes off the clock and included 26-yard runs by Michel and Rex Burkhead.

It was a workmanlike conclusion for the Patriots (14-5), whose losses all came away from New England. They beat the top two offenses in the Chiefs and Rams (15-4) in the postseason, and tied Pittsburgh for most Super Bowl titles.

The Patriots were terrific all game on defense, allowing the fewest points in a Super Bowl (tied with Dallas in 1972 against Miami).

"We're a relentless team," linebacker Dont'a Hightower said. "We didn't give up. A lot was thrown at us. When we play like we did tonight, we can't be beat."

The Rams, who reached the NFL championship game with the aid of a major officiating error in the conference title victory at New Orleans, never really threatened to reach the end zone.

"Last time I checked, defense wins championships," Rams running back C.J. Anderson said.

At 66, Bill Belichick became the oldest winning Super Bowl coach. The Patriots beat the Rams, then representing St. Louis, to begin their dynastic run in the 2002 game. They also have beaten Carolina and Philadelphia (2004 and `05, the last repeater); the

ABOVE: Los Angeles Rams linebacker Cory Littleton, right, intercepts a pass intended for Patriots receiver Chris Hogan, left, during the first half.
DAVID J. PHILLIP / AP PHOTO

OPPOSITE: Patriots quarterback Tom Brady fumbles as he is tackled by the Rams defensive linemen John Franklin-Myers (94) and Ethan Westbrooks (95) during first half action.
CHARLIE RIEDEL / AP PHOTO

WORLD CHAMPIONS

Seahawks in 2015; and the Falcons in 2017 in the only overtime in Super Bowl history.

They have lost three times, including to Philadelphia a year ago. New England is the first team since the 1972 Dolphins to win a Super Bowl the year after losing one.

How the Patriots accomplished it was atypical. The 10-point margin was their biggest in winning a championship.

Brady, who has won four Super Bowl MVP trophies, wasn't particularly sharp -- except when throwing to Edelman. He was the steadiest offensive player on the field, finishing with 10 catches for 141 yards.

"He played the best game of the year," Brady said. "He's a fighter. I'm just so proud of him. He's been an incredible player for this team."

In a season that opened with a suspension, Edelman closed a championship run as the MVP of Super Bowl LIII. Edelman is the seventh wide receiver to earn Super Bowl MVP honors and the first since Santonio Holmes in Super Bowl XLIII.

"[I] was just trying to get open.... I was asked to make a couple plays, and we were able to do that," Edelman said. "The defense was unreal. ... It's pretty crazy. They should be MVP on D."

"[It's] pretty surreal to be named MVP. Tough times don't last. Tough people do," Edelman said. "I preach that. ... I have to try to live to that. "

It just matters that we won," Edelman said. "It was a crazy year. We had a resilient bunch of guys."

Brady passed Charles Haley to become the only player with six Super Bowl titles.

All those suspicions about the Patriots declining this

ABOVE: Super Bowl LIII MVP Julian Edelman outruns a Rams defender to pick up extra yards during second half action.

OPPOSITE: Patriots linebacker Dont'a Hightower, top, breaks through to sack Rams quarterback Jared Goff.

Tight end Rob Gronkowski hauls in a 29-yard fourth quarter reception that made it first and goal at the Rams 2.
DAVID J. PHILLIP / AP PHOTO

season became moot as the defense made the 24-year-old Goff look awful and turned All-Pro running back Todd Gurley into a nonfactor.

While it was anything but odd to see New England celebrate a championship, the manner it earned this one was startling. The 2 1/2-point favorite Patriots moved the ball well, ran down the clock, but made uncharacteristic gaffes on offense. Goff and the Rams made more.

LA's second-ranked offense managed just 57 total yards for the half. The Rams were completely overmatched on the line and were particularly unable to handle the elusive Edelman, who had seven receptions for 93 yards.

Coach Sean McVay, whose Rams never had been blanked in a first half, let out a long, deep sigh just before halftime, recognizing how badly his team was manhandled, even though it trailed just 3-0. McVay, the youngest Super Bowl head coach at 34, admitted he was outcoached.

"I'm pretty numb right now, but definitely I got outcoached," McVay said. "I didn't do nearly a good enough job for our football team. ... This one is going to stick with you. It just stings in your gut."

McVay had no answers as Gurley, coming off knee issues, managed 35 yards rushing, Goff went 19 for 38 for 229 yards and was sacked four times.

"It's the toughest loss I ever had," Goff said. "It kills. It's terrible. It's a game I wish I would have played better. I wish I could have a million plays back."

Patriots owner Robert Kraft in a postgame interview called Brady "definitely the greatest player of all time, not just quarterback," citing his leadership and connection with teammates who are nearly half his age. Of Belichick, he said, "He's the GOAT of coaches, just like our quarterback is the GOAT of quarterbacks. And no one can dispute it after winning a sixth Super Bowl championship."

ABOVE: Stephen Gostkowski kicks a field goal to ice the game. The Pats called a timeout and considered going for it on 4th and 1 up 10-3 but instead chose to kick the field goal. Ryan Allen holds on the play.

MATT ROURKE / DAILY NEWS VIA AP PHOTO

OPPOSITE: New England Patriots' Sony Michel (26) dives over the goal line for the only touchdown of the game.

DAVID J. PHILLIP / AP PHOTO

BOX SCORE

	1	2	3	4	T
NEW ENGLAND	0	3	0	10	13
L.A. RAMS	0	0	3	0	3

Patriots Roster 2018-2019

#	NAME	POS.	HT.	WT.	AGE	EXP.	COLLEGE
83	Dwayne Allen	TE	6-3	265	28	7	Clemson
6	Ryan Allen	P	6-2	220	28	6	Louisiana Tech
80	Stephen Anderson	TE	6-2	230	26	3	California
60	David Andrews	C	6-3	300	26	4	Georgia
12	Tom Brady	QB	6-4	225	41	19	Michigan
90	Malcom Brown	DL	6-2	320	25	4	Texas
77	Trent Brown	OL	6-8	380	25	4	Florida
34	Rex Burkhead	RB	5-10	215	28	6	Nebraska
70	Adam Butler	DL	6-4	300	24	2	Vanderbilt
61	Marcus Cannon	OL	6-6	335	30	8	Texas Christian
49	Joe Cardona	LS	6-3	245	26	4	Navy
23	Patrick Chung	S	5-11	215	31	10	Oregon
94	Adrian Clayborn	DE	6-3	280	30	8	Iowa
35	Keion Crossen	DB	5-10	185	22	R	Western Carolina
58	Keionta Davis	DL	6-3	280	24	1	Tennessee-Chattanooga
29	Duke Dawson Jr.	DB	5-10	198	23	R	Florida
46	James Develin	FB	6-3	255	30	6	Brown
13	Phillip Dorsett	WR	5-10	192	26	4	Miami (Fla.)
43	Nate Ebner	DB	6-0	215	30	7	Ohio State
11	Julian Edelman	WR	5-10	198	32	10	Kent State
66	James Ferentz	OL	6-2	300	29	3	Iowa
98	Trey Flowers	DL	6-2	265	25	4	Arkansas
24	Stephon Gilmore	CB	6-1	202	28	7	South Carolina
3	Stephen Gostkowski	K	6-1	215	35	13	Memphis
87	Rob Gronkowski	TE	6-6	268	29	9	Arizona
93	Lawrence Guy	DL	6-4	315	28	8	Arizona State
21	Duron Harmon	DB	6-1	205	28	6	Rutgers
54	Dont'a Hightower	LB	6-3	260	28	7	Alabama
15	Chris Hogan	WR	6-1	210	31	6	Monmouth (N.J.)
2	Brian Hoyer	QB	6-2	216	33	10	Michigan State
50	Ramon Humber	LB	5-11	232	31	10	North Dakota State
27	J.C. Jackson	DB	6-1	198	23	R	Maryland
31	Jonathan Jones	DB	5-10	190	25	3	Auburn
97	Ufomba Kamalu	DL	6-6	295	26	3	Miami (Fla.)
75	Ted Karras	OL	6-4	305	25	3	Illinois
36	Brandon King	LB	6-2	220	25	4	Auburn
69	Shaq Mason	OL	6-1	310	25	4	Georgia Tech
59	Albert McClellan	LB	6-2	235	32	8	Marshall
32	Devin McCourty	DB	5-10	195	31	9	Rutgers
30	Jason McCourty	CB	5-11	195	31	10	Rutgers
22	Obi Melifonwu	DB	6-4	224	24	2	Connecticut
26	Sony Michel	RB	5-11	215	23	R	Georgia
84	Cordarrelle Patterson	WR	6-2	228	27	6	Tennessee
95	Derek Rivers	DE	6-5	250	24	2	Youngstown State
52	Elandon Roberts	LB	6-0	238	24	3	Houston
71	Danny Shelton	DL	6-2	345	25	4	Washington
55	John Simon	DE	6-2	260	28	6	Ohio State
18	Matthew Slater	WR	6-0	205	33	11	UCLA
62	Joe Thuney	OL	6-5	308	26	3	North Carolina State
53	Kyle Van Noy	LB	6-3	250	27	5	Brigham Young
68	LaAdrian Waddle	OL	6-6	315	27	6	Texas Tech
28	James White	RB	5-10	205	27	5	Wisconsin
91	Deatrich Wise Jr.	DL	6-5	275	24	2	Arkansas

Reserve/Injured

#	NAME	POS.	HT.	WT.	AGE	EXP.	COLLEGE
51	Ja'Whaun Bentley	LB	6-2	255	22	R	Purdue
14	Braxton Berrios	WR	5-9	190	23	R	Miami
33	Jeremy Hill	RB	6-1	230	26	5	LSU
47	Jacob Hollister	TE	6-4	245	25	2	Wyoming
85	Ryan Izzo	TE	6-5	255	23	R	Florida State
67	Ulrick John	OL	6-5	312	26	5	Georgia State
25	Eric Rowe	DB	6-1	205	26	4	Utah
44	Christian Sam	LB	6-2	240	22	R	Arizona State
63	Brian Schwenke	OL	6-3	318	27	6	California
76	Isaiah Wynn	OL	6-2	310	23	R	Georgia